Speak Truthfully

Speak Your Way to an Authentic Life with Awareness, Courage, and Confidence

ROBERT RABBIN

Published by Robert Rabbin
Los Angeles, California USA
news@authenticityaccelerator.com
www.authenticityaccelerator.com

An earlier edition of this book was published in 2008 under the title *RealTime Speaking: YOU are the Message!* This edition is significantly different: title, focus, front matter, and essays.

Book cover and interior design by Jane Green of Everlasting Magic Design.
design@everlastingmagic.com
www.everlastingmagicdesign.com

ISBN: 978-0-9871076-0-2

for O. B.
with whom my human heart opened

My heartfelt gratitude, love, and respect go to:

The 21 contributors to this book. Their courage to speak truthfully with authenticity and vulnerability inspires us all to find within ourselves an equivalent confidence, courage, and freedom. They demonstrate in unique and universal ways the wildly creative and cosmically powerful possibilities of self-expression;

To the hundreds of people who have participated in Speak Truthfully programs, affirming in so many different ways that speaking truthfully is an intrinsic human need and capacity;

Özlem Beldan, for her profound and moving Introduction; she is a magnificent ambassador of truthful speaking;

Shakaya Leone for her beautiful and heartfelt Foreword; Shakaya's sons, Landon and Liam, for spending so much time helping their mom write her Foreword;

Jane Green, for her many contributions to this book and my various websites;

Sherrie Hatfield, for years of deep friendship;

Jasmine Beldan, for being so indiscriminate in sharing her youthful exuberance and joy and for bringing happiness to everyone she meets.

Table of Contents

Foreword

Shakaya Leone

Raccontami una storia! That's Italian for "Tell me a story!" I love that, don't you?

Traditionally, grandmothers, mothers, sisters, women, and men of every culture have told their stories, passing them along the sacred web of life.

Sharing our story sends tiny green shoots suddenly sprouting within and all around us. And, our story can light the spark for a thousand others to grow new life, too!

But, when we don't share our story we can become ungrounded and lose connection to ourself and others; what we hide breeds underground, spawning roots that can strangle our creativity, power, and true beauty.

What I know about being a woman is that what we share won't harm another, but what we don't share is killing us.

The stories in this book map out each teller's prison escape route that leads to their freedom, and guide us to ours. That is the beauty of stories, and the ones you'll read here won't be forgotten anytime soon.

Let me tell you the story of how I met Robert, and the mayhem and miracles that have ensued since. I have interviewed some of the most famous luminaries on the planet, with a desire to draw out of them stories we won't find in their books or on the internet. They are all interview pros with perfectly prepared answers to expected questions, so I'd try to catch them right out of the gate with a simple question that would very often bring them to the edge of tears. "Tell me about your childhood, about the little girl/boy before you were who you are today. What was it like for you?" This is the game-changer. Whenever they would go there, to that tender spot where they were vulnerable and real rather than all polished and shiny and interview ready, I knew a very magical interview was about to unfold.

Life needs very few ingredients to be delicious. Vulnerability is one.

I happened to listen to an interview with one author, Robert, that so enchanted me. It was like that exciting moment when you hear your favorite song come on the radio — before iPods that could be programmed to play it any old time — and I literally stopped everything and just listened. And within minutes I heard myself whisper to my nearby aloe plant, "This is life-changing."

After that radio show I immediately sought out and devoured his book. Robert says, "Our speaking tells the true story of who we are and how we live. If we are to live a true life, a vibrant and vivid life, then our speaking will reveal, rather than conceal, our heart — the truth of who we are, what we are doing, and what we stand for."

Those words caused something to stir wildly inside me. So I did what I always do when I wish to embody a new dream: I slept with them under my pillow.

They sent shakti through my crown burning fear into fuel for the journey of transformation I didn't even know had been activated.

That is when I met my inner Slavegirl.

The Slavegirl is a shadow archetype that lives in many women. When I discovered my shadow stealing my dreams, allowing me to settle for less than what I know my heart and soul desire, convincing me I was undeserving of beauty and luxury, I wanted to banish her!

But Robert's intoxicating words had me craving that magical elixir of authenticity, which I knew would be out of reach if I rejected any part of myself; I would never truly be free, beautiful or able to live my legacy by hiding or repressing. So I explored my shadow instead and found seeds of exquisite gifts, like pearls that start out from something unbeautiful.

Robert says, "Speaking Truthfully is how we bring what is inside, outside. This is how we mark the world with our presence. Speaking Truthfully is not about being right. It is about being real."

Wanting to be real, not right, urged me to dive deep and discover buried treasures of my own mythology. Who am I really? What inspires me? How can I live a legendary life?

Robert says, "I believe we all want a vibrant, meaningful life, one in which we can dream big and make things happen. We want to live inspired lives. to light up the world with that inner spark of magic that is ours alone — our authentic self."

I love that. Even though it can feel scary to speak our truth and share our story, I have found the parts we think are our imperfections, the ones we try to hide, are what makes us loveable. We are most beautiful when we are authentic.

So, inspired by both Robert and my Slavegirl, I turned the tables on myself and wrote a blog about my story that centered on a secret fantasy I've had for decades. At the time it felt like a risk to be so vulnerable; as it turns out that was the safest thing I could have done! I tapped into a well of creativity inside myself that gave me a unique voice in my community. I now attract and support superstar women who also want to live full-bodied legendary lives!

Robert's books, especially this one, are North Stars lighting our path. I might not have found my way to that blog otherwise. And months later, that experience evolved into a ceremonial birthday celebration where I invited my inner Slavegirl and other women friends to hold space for me to step into a new archetype: The Empress. She is helping me write a new story for myself, my fairytale.

Speaking my truth seems to fill us all with an irresistible aroma, an alluring blend of confidence and heart-mending connection to our authentic self and others.

For me, anything else is living in an empty castle.

Introduction

Özlem Beldan

"If you shut up truth and bury it underground, it will but grow."
Emile Zola

As I sit here writing, I'm wondering what it costs to sacrifice one choice for another. In spirituality this is better known as Karma, the cause and effect of our choices and actions. If we do *this*, then *that* follows. But if we do *that*, then something else happens. With each choice, there is an opportunity cost: we pay the price of what we didn't choose.

But today, in particular, I'm wondering what it costs to sacrifice your truth, to betray yourself and not speak truthfully. I wonder what price we pay for choosing to bury our truth in fear of disappointing our family, our parents, our community, our society. I wonder what price we pay to fulfill others' expectations while we abandon the truth of our heart. I wonder what price we pay for choosing to be one of the crowd rather than our own unique self.

I have often read that nothing happens in isolation. It is said that if you change just one thing then everything changes. I wonder how my life would be different had I not been afraid to speak the truth, had I not betrayed my heart. I wonder how my life would be different had I spoken up each time I was afraid of the opinions of others, afraid of being wrong, and afraid of being ostracized by a community for being or thinking differently. It's hard to say what might have happened, but I know what would not have happened. I wouldn't have developed a veil to hide behind, allowing my true self to become invisible, and I wouldn't have developed digestive disorders that every healer I have been to has told me is due to self-suppression. I wouldn't have been estranged from my self, not the ego self that is so pedantic and insistent about trying to be perfect, but my real self, the one that is perfectly unique, and therefore real — my authentic self, the one I am here to share with the world.

It's taken me so long to see that living is about growing, that it's about accepting my own unique looking glass through which to view the world. It's taken me so long to find my own voice with which to contribute and share my unique take on life. It's taken me so long to find that the essence of my life is not about concealing but about revealing my true self. It's taken me so long to not be afraid of others and to not to hide my truth from the world. It's taken me so long to be able to speak with out fear, and to realize my life is not necessarily about being right or wrong; but it is about "being." There are no medals for hiding from yourself or shrinking in front of others. There are no awards for swallowing truth in fear of what others might say.

My favorite poet, Rumi, says, "There's a place out beyond right and wrong; I'll meet you there." I've been so afraid of speaking up that I haven't had the courage to venture to this place that Rumi speaks of so beautifully. It's always sounded like some never-never land, a nirvana. My fears of being wrong, of being different, and of being judged have stopped me from meeting the world with my truth. My fear estranged me from my voice, my authentic voice that comes from my authentic self, my heart.

But after all these years and all these fears, I found the greatest courage to live life more fully when I learned to see myself. Once I learned to stop hiding from myself and to stop hiding that true self from the world, my life changed. In Robert Rabbin's Speak Truthfully program, this is called "to see, and be seen," and it was a powerful turning point for me after years of hiding. It was through this program that I found my voice and started to connect with my truth and my true self, which I had hidden all these years.

I found that when I am not trying to be right and not afraid of being wrong, Rumi's playground does exist. In fact, it's where life happens, it's where we grow and flourish and find the joy in our living and being. It's where we shine. It's where we come alive.

In this playground, beyond being right or wrong, my veil dropped and I started to speak truthfully. I stopped hiding from life. My self-suppression, my true heart that had been buried for so long, began to surface, to be seen, to be acknowledged, to be healed, and slowly my chronic digestive disorder began to heal.

And so, dear reader, I wonder what truth you may have buried inside of you. I wonder about the cost of that; what price have you paid to not speak your truth? I wonder what is growing, yearning to be released, to be spoken, to be unveiled, so that you may be reunited with that true "self" that has been there all along. I wonder what treasures await within you.

May this book inspire you to unveil the places in your life where you may still be hiding your authentic self, your unique beauty, your unique heart and soul, your unique voice. I hope you find your unique voice so you can let the world truly hear you. Most importantly, let yourself hear you, perhaps for the very first time, and when you do, enjoy playing in Rumi's playground, in the land beyond right and wrong.

I'll meet you there.

Preface

Robert Rabbin

Speaking Truthfully is how we bring what is deep inside, outside. This is how we mark the world with our authentic presence. This is how we announce and represent our authentic self to others. Speaking Truthfully reveals, rather than conceals, our authentic purpose, intentions, and motives; it shows the strength of our spine and quality of our character. Speaking Truthfully comes through our mouth, but from our heart.

Speaking itself is more than our verbal and non-verbal communications. It is bigger and broader in scope and meaning: speaking is how we move in and through life. Our speaking is our life; our life is our speaking. Someone once asked me in a workshop if one could speak authentically without living authentically. I said no. Speaking Truthfully is not a light switch we flick when it suits us; we can't hire a speech writer to craft an "authentic" message if we are not living authentically. St. Francis of Assisi is quoted as saying, "It's no use walking anywhere to preach unless our walking is our preaching."

To live an authentic life, we have to Speak Truthfully. To Speak Truthfully, we have to live an authentic life. We cannot hide from or be afraid of what we truly want to say, need to say. We cannot hide from what others might say when we reveal the truth of our heart. We cannot sleep at night in the darkness of unspoken secrets. And just as we have to tell the truth of our inner life, we have to tell the truth of our outer life: we have to own up to what we do, to our actions. This is integrity. This truth-telling about the inside and the outside is how we energize our authentic life with integrity, with wholeness and wholeheartedness.

Why do we hide? Why don't we Speak Truthfully? Telling the truth is risky business. Many of us found out as children that telling the truth can get us into trouble. So we learn how to obscure and spin the truth for approval, security, acceptance, to get what we want, to avoid punishment. We condition ourselves to distort our truth, so much so that we often don't know what is true about our own life.

Telling the truth requires practice. We have to learn how to get in touch with our truth, and then we have to become fearless enough to speak it. This is the only way we will find out that truth has the power to liberate, to enliven, to empower — to free us from fear, shame, guilt, and the opinions of others. Speaking Truthfully is how we discover that we need not fear truth, that we can live authentically and safely in truth.

Almost everyone who comes to my programs is afraid to stand in public and speak their truth. To speak our truth means to show ourself, not our "knowing." It means to show our soul, not the red tape we have accumulated in the form of experiences, skills, knowledge, ideas, and beliefs. It means being seen by people without defense or pretense, without fear of their criticism and judgment, without hiding. When we stand in front of others, we are exposing ourselves completely. This total vulnerability triggers every one of our insecurities and fears, including the fear of not being good enough, or right enough. I am not talking about being good or right enough to speak well; I mean good and right enough as a human being. We fear being the one that some celestial quality-control angel will point to and say, Not good enough! In contrast to this fear, another fear people have is of their own beauty and brilliance!

Speaking Truthfully is about living out loud, about liberating the full measure of our creative power and expressive potential. If we do not first free our speaking spirit from the repressive tyranny of self-doubt and self-suppression, we will never find the song only we can sing, and all our speaking will be off-key and flat. And so will our life be off-key and flat, and our great dreams and aspirations will remain unspoken, dying, or dead within us. But if we reclaim our power of Speaking Truthfully, then something huge and wonderful happens, magically and mysteriously, almost inevitably. When we Speak Truthfully, we create our authentic life one word at a time. Speaking Truthfully is a wish-fulfilling tree, whose gifts and blessings are many, including profound self-knowledge, intimacy with others, personal credibility, leadership believability, professional impeccability — it's all in Speaking Truthfully.

I moved from the U.S. to Australia in October 2005, where I lived until May 2011. Shortly after I arrived in Melbourne, I founded RealTime Speaking and offered a variety of programs focusing on public speaking and authentic self-expression. (That company continues to thrive with licensed facilitators, while I now conduct exclusive Speak Truthfully programs as part of the Authenticity Accelerator.) The philosophy, principles, and practices of these programs were derived from my own style of public speaking, which blossomed from 30 years of study and practice in personal growth, meditation, and self-inquiry. Yes, I was on that road to self-realization. After fulfilling my longing to know myself, I was left with an unexpected new mountain to climb: authentic self-expression, or Speaking Truthfully. Self-realization does not automatically become authentic self-expression. Inner knowledge of the self does not give us a free pass to Speak Truthfully. We have to learn this, practice this, do this.

I've worked with all kinds of people, including politicians and corporate executives, non-profit managers and musicians, educators and entrepreneurs, professional speakers and business coaches, holistic healers and spiritual teachers, authors and escorts. People come for their own reasons to learn to speak truthfully. Some people come to learn to speak more freely, in order to be better able to sell a product, promote their business, to give talks, to stand in front of media microphones. Some want to be better leaders, and they know their leadership credibility comes from their *speaking*, from who they are, not from their title, position, or PowerPoint presentation. Some want to be better at teaching or running workshops or meetings. Some want to be better fund-raisers. Some want to be able to say hard things to people close to them, things that are risky because they are so nakedly real and true, and which may rock the boat of complacency. Some want to speak their visions and dreams without fear of failure or rejection.

But underneath all these reasons is something else, something equally profound. It is spiritual. It is a longing for integrity of being, for wholeness, for authenticity and truth. I received the following email in July 2007, which is symbolic of the spiritual longing, the existential *need*, people have to speak freely:

Hello Robert,
I have read through the course information for Speak Truthfully and was wondering if you consider the course as life changing? It sounds very powerful, or perhaps I just want it to be so. I have always been quite shy, and anxiety sometimes shuts me down. I fear group speaking and being the center of attention more than anything. I'm tired of this though. I would like to just be myself, at all times and in any situation, and not feel like my mind or my heart shuts down due to some form of stress. I like what you say and many things ring true to me, but I want to know if I can expect a great shift in my approach to communication with people. This is very important to me now, as I'm tired of feeling weak and closed off from myself, from other people, and from the life that seems to pass me by because I do not speak up when opportunities knock. It feels that something in me is dying, day by day, and only if I let it out will it, and possibly myself, survive.

In every workshop, people want to reclaim their lost power of self-expression, they want to heal their wounds of self-doubt and restore their creative vitality from the clutches of repressive self-censoring. They quickly agree with me when I tell them that full and free self-expression is our natural state! People are finding the courage and confidence to speak from their hearts. They are healing themselves of criticism-induced and judgment-inflicted wounds to their creative and expressive inner being. They are discovering a practical enlightenment, a freedom to bring their deepest self, their truest longings and dreams and aspirations out into the light of day. No longer afraid to see and be seen, they now stand without pretense or defense in their truth, speaking with authenticity and vulnerability, in full and honest connection with others. This is a kind of miracle, I think. Finding their true voice and the confidence to speak with that voice brings each to a state of grace, and in so doing they become a blessing to you and me and to our world. We are all the better for this.

Almost from the beginning, I wanted to write a book about Speak Truthfully, in part to share what I've learned about speaking truthfully in public during my twenty years of doing so; in part to show how public speaking can be a means to professional excellence and distinction, as well as a way of personal growth and spiritual self-realization; and in part to share the profound and poignant stories of people I've been honored to work with.

After several false starts, I got it. As Edward R. Murrow once said, "The obscure we see eventually, the completely apparent takes longer." What I finally realized was that the book needed to be a collaboration between me and workshop participants! The book wanted more than just my voice and perspective; it wanted a diversity of voices, perspectives, experiences, and applications.

I wrote an invitation and emailed it out to everyone with whom I had worked. Submissions came from grandparents, mothers, fathers, wives, husbands, daughters, sons, nephews and nieces; from corporate managers, school principals, barristers, authors, leadership experts, musicians, spiritual teachers, life coaches, holistic healers, entrepreneurs, opera singers; from many different spiritual and religious affiliations; and from the rainbow spectrum of sexual orientations: straight, gay, lesbian, bi, still-experimenting-and-as-yet-undecided. It is the variety of styles and voices of the contributors that so richly flavors this book, just as their searing candor and disarming disclosures spice it with humanity and dignity.

Most of the contributors had never written anything for publication before. For a few, English is their second language. With utmost editorial restraint, I tried to not modulate anyone's voice or moderate their story. I cared less for literary and grammatical perfection, preferring to retain the rhythm and syntax of their "speaking." Each contributor had final approval of their essay.

After each essay, I wrote a Commentary to expand upon an experience, principle, or idea from the preceding essay. My Commentaries reflect many of the themes I discuss with people in workshops, having to do with public speaking, self-expression, freedom, integrity, authenticity, joy, humor, fearlessness, confidence, tenderness, and passion.

The stories in this book are at once unique and universal, each one describing, in 300 words or 2,000, a hero's journey to a place of self-blessing and re-enchantment, to a place of power and passion, tenderness and tears. In these pages, the speakers strip away their masks and roles, often revealing things aloud and publicly for the first time ever, strengthened by a new confidence to claim their rightful place in life, to stand and speak with dignity and honor, to embody the vast flows of life-force which move through each of us, animating and enlivening our precious few moments, beautifying creation with our truthful voice, a unique song which must be expressed without fear, shame, or embarrassment!

It is now my pleasure to invite you to turn the page, and begin your own hero's journey to self-blessing. May you find inspiration and guidance in these pages to experience the fullness of your own inner beauty and the courage and confidence to express what only you can express: YOU.

Speak Truthfully

Shame Is Not The Ultimate Reality

Carla van Raay

Readers might know of me as the author of *God's Callgirl*, the memoir of a Catholic girl who first became a nun and then, four years after leaving the convent at the age of 30, decided to become a prostitute. Since then, I have faced many demons and experienced deep healing from the legacy of a dismal and abusive childhood, the story of which I have shared in my book.

I came to Robert's weekend workshop in high spirits. For three years, I had been speaking to groups of people who wanted to better understand my story, to find inspiration to heal themselves. My trepidation and nervousness at being in front of a crowd was gradually replaced with excitement and pleasure. Even so, I was apt to blush for very little reason and this annoyed me. I mentioned this at the workshop as something I wanted to address.

I was not expecting nor prepared for what suddenly came up for me during the weekend course! Late on the first day, I was overwhelmed with the discovery that my blushing had to do with a deep feeling of shame. This feeling went back all the way to very early childhood. It had been there for so long that it had etched its way into my psyche in layers, because I had definitely dealt with shame before. I had now unearthed an unexpectedly deep layer that I had never experienced or acknowledged before. As it came up during the workshop, I didn't recognize it as a "layer." I felt only shame and couldn't feel anything else! I felt that the *core of my being was shame* and that this had been true all the time, even while I had been recounting my story to people. *I felt like a fake*. I felt like a fake because I had been talking over the top of this feeling, standing on the shame-as-my-core-identity without even knowing it. I had been talking over the top of this feeling even as I was talking to my audience about facing feelings completely!

I was devastated to discover myself to be a fake. My whole self-awareness was swallowed up by this conviction, and I couldn't move.

At the end of Saturday's session, Robert came to speak to me about what was going on with me. He told me a simple truth that I couldn't see in my disturbed state, in more or less the following words: "If you can see your shame, if you can name it, look at it, and if you can call yourself a fake, then this is not the ultimate truth of who you are. The ultimate truth of who you are is the one who can see this and acknowledge this."

That's when things changed. Immediately after Robert said that, I gained enough distance from my feelings and thoughts to see that shame was not my core identity. Even more than that, I once again felt the true innocence of my being, only this time in an even clearer way! I cried tears of sheer relief and gratitude.

Ever since then, speaking has become so much more of a joy. Yes, I continue to feel all sorts of things, but I no longer tell myself that these fleeting feelings define or determine my true self. I acknowledge the feeling or thought that is there and then present the highest truth I know, without interference from the thoughts or feelings.

This change in perspective is not something that I can lose. Once something has been seen for what it is, it loses its power. Thank you, Robert, for helping me over a huge hump and facilitating such a profound insight!

Commentary

"I want to acknowledge you, I want to announce you, as no one ever has before ..."
Rainer Maria Rilke

Carla is an international best-selling author, and a woman who has spent her entire life investigating and illuminating the physical, emotional, mental, and spiritual facets of her being. She is an intrepid explorer of truth. She seeks to dismantle defenses so as to live luxuriously with herself — and in relationship. As with so many others I have met in these workshops, Carla displays a courage and determination to become free and fully self-expressive that is truly amazing.

When Carla walked in the workshop room on Sunday, the morning after the incident she describes, I had to look twice to recognize her. She was radiant and glowing and bright. She had a saintly aura, in the sense that she emanated a profound peace and inner stability.

I did say something along the lines of, "If you can see your shame, if you can name it, look at it, and if you can call yourself a fake, then this is not the ultimate truth of who you are. The ultimate truth of who you are is the one who can see this and acknowledge this." But I wasn't speaking dogmatically, I was simply listening to her and responding. I know from my own experience that we are not the objects of our awareness, we are awareness itself. But I wasn't trying to teach her, or you, this rather esoteric tidbit. I was just being present with her, listening. Then I spoke, connected to myself and to her. She was so in the seeing of her shame and yet also wanting to get out. She made me say just the right thing to free her. It was really her own speaking and her own knowing that she conjured through me. This is the value of connection, and of listening. Our speaking becomes modified, sometimes even created from scratch, by what we take in from deep within ourselves and from our audience and from the whole environment in which we are speaking. Listening, feeling, connection — these produce a magical, alchemical speaking.

I felt close to Carla. We seemed in some ways to have traveled similar paths. I spent as many years in an ashram as Carla spent in a convent. She read the Bible. I read the sacred texts of Vedanta and Kashmir Shaivism. We both meditated and courted silence through contemplation. She left the convent and I left the ashram. In the workshop, Carla helped me understand why and how public speaking has become my spiritual path. It's so damn real and exposed, exposing and challenging at a visceral, instead of a mystical, level. There is no hiding, as one can hide on a meditation cushion, or in a community of like-minded people. Public speaking does not permit us to be smug or complacent, at least not the way I do it and teach it. We do not settle into certainties, ours or someone else's. We challenge ourselves to be more authentic, more expressive, more transparent. We listen to ourselves as we speak, to what we are saying and how we are saying it. We listen also to the place from where we speak. That's the real listening, that's the transformative listening. *Where are these words coming from?*

If we are as sincere and brave as Carla, then our listening becomes so acute, so deft, that we begin to hear and feel these deep contractions, "I felt that the *core of my being was shame*." All her success and notoriety, she says, was built upon this core identity. But her sincerity and bravery also lead her deeper, beyond the contraction and conflict to the resolution, "I once again felt the true innocence of my being." She discovered that she need not be determined or defined by shame, or guilt, or anger; and this insight carried her to depths and dimensions of joy and release and relief. In these new currents she now swims, with tears of joy mingling with the salt of the sea.

We are all in this struggle, aren't we? Aren't we all seeking to recover our true innocence of being, not as an idea or hope, not as a borrowed concept or deep-dish dogma, but as a felt and lived personal experience?

This is why I think public speaking is not about techniques or skills; it is about authenticity. And authenticity is a way of being, a way of living, a commitment to speak from as deep a place of truth as we can, each and every time, all the while being open to more, to seeing the barriers, the fears, the demons, the shames, whatever is in the way, OK, bring it up as I speak, in my speaking, so I can hear and feel that maybe yesterday's truth is today's falsehood, and let me find the strength and courage to go deeper, to speak truer, to find the tears and joys that await all of us when we stand up to speak our truth, truthfully, transparently.

Carla is a shadow digger, someone with enough guts to rummage in the darkness where her dispossessed and lost powers are, where terrible taboos reign supreme, where the wandering shattered parts of herself are waiting, waiting, waiting for just such guts to dig deep enough and long enough to find them and bring them back to the light, and herself to wholeness.

The Waldzell Moment

Laurent S. Labourmène

When the stakes are high, who are you going to be?

I turned 32 two days ago, on the 8th of August 2007. What a life it has been so far.

Before the age of 13, I experienced sexual, verbal, physical, and psychological abuse. From that beginning, I experienced a near fatal car accident, a loaded rifle shoved in my face, a life-threatening medical diagnosis, severe depression, and recurring thoughts of suicide. Until now, these were the silent unclaimed things within me.

Forget the metaphors. I have actually lived the Hell and Purgatory of Dante's *Divine Comedy*. I have that T-shirt and I have worn it so many times that the fabric is completely transparent now and you can see right through it, to my skin and beyond, right through to the very stuff that makes up my *me-ness*.

So I stand on the edge of what I am, a man climbing out of his fears, standing here raw before you, somehow rising above it all, naked and exposed for the entire world to see. This is not easy. Nor is it easy to stay hidden in fears.

It was 3:45 on Thursday, May 18, 2006. I will never forget the despair that descended upon me when my doctor told me I was HIV+. My world would never be the same again. That's how I began my very own divine comedy. The wind had been taken out of me. In the weeks and months that followed, any confidence I had in myself simply collapsed under the weight of the diagnosis. I was unable to find the strength within me to rise above it. I retreated more and more from the world in my personal life. But I was determined to complete a project I was working on, part of my dream to rebuild the world, believing that my inspiration for it was the only lifeline I had at the time. Without it, I felt I had no reason to live and I would have surely ended my life.

My dreams saved my life throughout this period. I also felt that by continuing to live my dream I could somehow make sense of everything that had happened to me, that there was some larger purpose to this hell that I was in, and while I didn't know it yet, my dreams would help me one day see the order of things in the apparent chaos that was consuming my life. So I drowned myself even deeper in my professional life and the international foundation for young global leaders I had established some four years before.

I felt that the future of leadership was a matter of authenticity, vulnerability, empathy — being able to get real and speak from a truthful, transparent place. I felt that our leaders needed to be as adept at surrendering themselves to this place of authenticity as they are at innovating initiatives of breathtaking power. This was my journey too. Throughout this entire period I had been undergoing my own profound transformation in leadership, trying to adjust to the health news I had received.

At around this time, I received news that I was one of 12 emerging leaders from around the world named "Architect of the Future" by Paulo Coelho, the Brazilian writer and author of *The Alchemist*, and a global jury of the Austrian-based Waldzell Institute. The name "Waldzell" derives from a fictitious place in Hermann Hesse's novel *The Glass Bead Game* where selected people, once a year, speak one universal language, enabling the possibility for a true deep dialogue. Its effect reaches far beyond the circle of players and essentially contributes to the evolution of the planet.

I was also invited to make a presentation about the work that I was doing in the field of leadership at the Waldzell Institute's Global Meeting, an intimate annual gathering of 150 world leaders and Nobel Laureates in September. The venue was just outside of Vienna in one of the world's oldest Benedictine monasteries, Melk Abbey. In the course of its history, the Benedictine abbey of Melk has inspired architects, painters, scientists, and writers such as Umberto Eco, who wrote the novel *The Name of the Rose*. So it wasn't your typical venue or presentation by any means. I could feel the challenges of place and purpose calling me to a place of truth that, given my recent diagnosis, was terrifying to consider.

I asked Robert Rabbin to assist me in preparing the presentation. We first connected by email in early 2006, when Robert commented on the work I was doing: "Your work reminds me of a poem by Rumi, 'Start a huge foolish project like Noah, It makes absolutely no difference what people think of you.'" Like Dante's guide, Virgil, Robert came into my life and helped me navigate to the place where I can more confidently write about these tough things today. In the beginning I asked him: "Where is this Paradise and how do I get there?" For him there is only one answer. And like some Zen master playing with my worst fears to make some enlightened point, he laughed and simply said one word:

"SPEAK!"

I decided that rather than talk *about* authentic leadership, I was going to talk *from* a space of authenticity and my own experiences and my personal struggles with it. Robert encouraged me to use my talk to invite openness into this global gathering, to ask for a deeper dialogue and emotional connection with others, and to use my recent story and personal struggles as a bridge for me to step into this space myself. It was, after all, the very essence of the work that underpinned the foundation I was setting up. I worked with Robert over the course of a few weeks to draft a succinct presentation that would effectively allow me to model the type of leadership I was on about. I decided I had to talk from my place of greatest fear at a time when the stakes were the highest for me both personally and professionally, and lead from there, inviting others to do the same.

It was as if the decision to lead and speak from this space detonated an avalanche of accumulated silent things within me: all my fears, insecurities, and apprehensions. Added to this was a chorus of historic voices that emerged into the present moment: The man who sexually abused me at the age of seven, "Don't speak up, or you will be killed." Physical and verbal abuse throughout my childhood, "Don't speak up or we will put you up for adoption." Coming-out to my family about my sexuality, "Don't speak up or you will shame us and the family." A loaded shotgun in my face, "Don't speak up, or I will kill you and those closest to you."

Not only were these inner voices screaming at me, but so, too, were other voices, external ones, shouting me down. Some people felt threatened personally and professionally at the level of authenticity I was intending, the level of disclosure and nakedness I needed to display, in order for my soul to find new life. I was surrounded by a chorus of voices, internal and external, shouting "No, Laurent, you cannot speak. Be quiet! Do not speak."

What should I do? I was like Santiago in Paulo Coelho's book *The Alchemist*, trying to read the signs around me for some answer. And on Friday afternoon, like some chapter from that very same book, I came face to face with Paulo Coelho himself. And later that day, still undecided, I came face to face with one of the Waldzell Meeting's keynote speakers, Robert Gallo, the co-discoverer of the very virus that was flowing through my veins. The synchronicities were dizzying. I was overwhelmed.

And then Saturday came: the moment to make the presentation and speech. It was one of the hardest things I've had to do but I could not turn from Gaston Bachelard, and his caution about creating our own suffering: "What is the source of our first suffering? It lies in the fact that we hesitated to speak. It was born in the moment when we accumulated silent things within us."

So standing tall on the shoulders of my first sufferings, those times when I hesitated to speak, those moments when I had accumulated silent things within me, I decided to *speak* my truth. It felt like my first time. It was.

I don't think that we are truly born the day we leave our mother's womb and enter this world. Rather, we are born in the moments when we pass through the real life rites of passage and truly see the connections between things, the great purpose and order of things, and make the choice to express and lead from that deepest place within ourselves. In that moment we truly cross the bridge and enter this world and embody Life. In these moments we birth ourselves again and again.

So I spoke from this place inside me. The words were like little doorways into rabbit holes out of this world and deep into another world of integrity and truth, courage and transparency.

I now know that every second is a Waldzell moment waiting to happen. When the stakes are high, who will we be and what will we say?

They say the sea levels are rising. Yes, I know what Noah must have felt like. I have dedicated my life to building arcs not for animals, but for authenticity, vulnerability, intimacy, and love. Every day I try to venture beyond the backyard of myself, and into the wilderness and shadows of my being. I try to stop falling asleep on the job and at the wheel and anchor myself into the *all-ness* of who I am; no longer like a magpie picking out just the shiny bits for the entire world to see. I try to moor myself into both my *yin* and *yang*, allowing myself to be touched with the two hands of its fire and to lead from there. For this is all I know now. Anything else would feel like I was dead from the neck down.

In every moment we have the choice to catch up with the times and to drink freely from Rumi's cup. And when you do, I challenge you not to feel that you have been kissed on the lips and punched in the stomach all at the same time! For this is the Royal Academy, the great planetary training ground, the crucible and concourse through which all the fierce kick-ass movers and shakers have passed and honed their craft: our musicians, artists, scientists, philosophers, inventors, healers, writers, poets, saints, sages, entrepreneurs and leaders.

Like Gandhi, Martin Luther King, Nelson Mandela, and Aung San Suu Kyi, let those holy rubies within you tumble like mammoth avalanches from your beautiful, once parched mouth and shake you and this world to its very foundations!

So now I ask: Who are you going to be?

SPEAK!

We need more Noahs.

Commentary

"We fell morally ill because we became used to saying something different from what we thought."
Václav Havel

Laurent's essay speaks to the courage one needs to discover one's core, and to speak from that place of authenticity. It can be risky business: one may have to face daunting dark places and overcome tremendous terror. Getting as real with oneself as Laurent gets requires a warrior's spirit and heart, which he has. Courage is an elemental principle of Speak Truthfully.

You can see from Laurent's biography and its abbreviated list of his accomplishments that he is very bright, very educated, very talented; a true emerging global leader at only 32. But I am less impressed with these things than with his courage and heart, with his spirit, with his willingness to put everything on the line for one minute of truth, his truth, the simple standing and saying, "This is me. Here is what's happening. Here is what I see, and here is my dream."

Laurent has given me the great gift of seeing him up close and personal through the events he describes in his essay. He participated in two workshops, and we spent numerous hours in one-to-one meetings. He wept openly. He showed his fears, his terrors. He told me things he hadn't said to anyone, and I watched his body tremble from the intensity of the discharge.

Within the eye of these storms was, and is, a gentle, loving, caring soul, one with a vision for living, for leadership, that is predicated on vulnerability, honesty, empathy, transparency, and love. We had many conversations exploring this style of authentic living and leading, and we agreed that a telling distinction must be made, the one that separates those who speak *about* authentic leadership as distinct from those who speak *from* authentic leadership.

We agreed that there are plenty of people who had their models and theories and maps, and who could pontificate for hours *about* integral this and authentic that. But where is the new person, the one who would willingly go into the cave of inner demons and ancient fears and face them down, the demons that stand guard on our soul's desire to stand up against their threats and intimidations? Where is the person who could speak *from*, who knows that their actual life, their character and actions, are the message?

I know what it's like to believe in these inner voices that have threatened to kill us if we speak, if we tell, if we challenge corrupt power, if we dissent, if we just speak out. I lived with these voices for years, some real, some imaginary. It doesn't matter, because when we feel in our bones that we will be arrested, imprisoned, tortured, and killed for our speaking, when we can feel our knees being broken, our skin flaming and crackling in fires, these terrors are almost unbearable. Can we really risk all of that again, just to speak?

Yes. Otherwise, we are not alive. As Laurent says, we are truly born only when we pass through such a rite of passage, when we consciously claim our own soul and original voice. Until then, we are not really living.

Laurent is an inspiration, because he is willing to call up his terrors, face them squarely, and show and tell these things to anyone who is willing to look and listen. And then, from that cleared place within, from that deep, invincible place of vulnerability, where the individual intersects the collective, and where humanity becomes one in Life, where the wounds and fears are dissolved, he speaks.

It may not be easy to speak from this place, but the willingness to do so is what will get us there. In a word, it means to speak from one's depths, which is inspirational in the extreme. We don't hear many leaders today speak with the same ruthless candor as Laurent. We don't hear many leaders today speak of their struggles and triumphs to reach a place of authentic self-expression, a place somewhere down deep, inside. And yet, this is what we want, isn't it?

Many of the business leaders I've coached find it difficult to put *themselves* out front. They'd rather lead with their title, their knowledge, their accomplishments, their net worth, their positional power, their ability to intimidate. Where are *they*? When everything is stripped away, when the x-ray machine is scanning for their true heart, or their soul, what do we see?

I am not suggesting that one must disclose every single thing about how they live, to everyone, all the time. I'm not talking about revealing the minutiae of one's life indiscriminately. I am talking about revealing that *thing* in a person that we need to see in order to know them enough to trust them to be who they say they are. Years ago, I did a bit of rock climbing, enough to know that when it came time to pick your belay partner, the person to whom you were entrusting your life, you chose based on that *thing* in them that you could trust, their inner character that you knew would not betray the trust you were placing in them. If you didn't see it, if you didn't feel it, well, no thanks. It's no different with leadership. It's no different with public speaking. Cut the crap, and show your character.

I've always admired Václav Havel, playwright and former president of the Czech Republic, as an authentic person and leader. Mr. Havel echoes Laurent in setting a new standard for leadership.

"Without a global revolution in the sphere of human consciousness, nothing will change for the better ... and the catastrophe toward which this world is headed, whether it be ecological, social, demographic or a general breakdown of civilization, will be unavoidable. More and more people are realizing that the future of the human race on this earth rests increasingly in the hands of those who manage to not think of themselves alone, who act with regard for others. Yes, the future of humankind rests today with the civilization of spirit, responsibility and love. The only option is a change in the sphere of human conscience. It is not enough to invent new machines, new regulations, new institutions. We must develop a new understanding of the true purpose of our existence on this Earth."

The civilization of spirit, responsibility, and love is where Speak Truthfully comes from, an inner place we must all work to discover, and from where we must speak in order for our words to have true power, to be truly believable, to be worthy of our individual and collective spirit. If we do not speak from this place, all the clever, slick, and polished public speaking skills in the world will not help us to speak well, or truly.

Just Speak From Your Heart

Sherrie Hatfield

Through years of learning, developing skills, and acquiring knowledge to become the best I could be, I always found myself falling short, collapsing into a feeling of "something is missing" and a knowing that I am not really saying what is in my heart. When I am quiet, I always hear inspiring, uplifting, and truthful thoughts and feelings deep within. I have realized that my truest goal was to be able to express this inner beauty. In meeting Robert for the first time, at a talk in Sydney, I heard and saw my own inner heart and wisdom being expressed out loud and openly.

My background work has been working with children from six weeks to 12 years as a childcare educator. I have dedicated most of my teaching to re-learning with the children who we really are. At one point, I discovered that "education" comes from the Latin word *educare*, meaning "to bring out." This idea sent me on a new path of teaching. Most education is primarily focused on what we put *in* the kids, and suddenly I realized that education is also, even mostly, a matter of what we can *bring out* — their dormant creative impulses and desires.

Later, as an Inner Child practitioner, I explored with many clients the inner truth to our lives and makeup. To my utmost amazement (as well as my clients') there it all was — incredible wisdom already within us, waiting to be brought out. Time after time, each client discovered that they had their own answers and knowing right inside them, just waiting for the moment when they would truly *express* what they already knew! Most of the issues and conditions they were exploring were really limits they created and believed in and hung like a heavy curtain over their own greater wisdom. They knew how to resolve their own issues, but had forgotten that they knew!

I have experienced and experimented for years in this field and found, especially here in Australia, we do not openly express ourselves, our deepest thoughts and feelings, for fear of being truly seen and heard. We are afraid of what people will think, so we don't want to stand out. We certainly don't want to speak out! The pain and confusion which lived within my clients were their deepest unexpressed desires, and their regrets that they never felt heard, acknowledged, understood — or never said what they truly felt or thought, especially in their relationships. Again and again I would come to this same place of sadness and frustration with clients, with myself, seemingly caught in a maze of illusions from which we couldn't escape into the truth of who we felt we could be.

In the first talk I heard Robert give, I saw in action something that I had been trying to find. He spoke softly yet clearly and with such compassion, with joy and conviction about what he was sharing. He spoke words that were inspiring and thought provoking, with such a beauty that I knew I had finally seen in action what I had been looking for all these years.

It was only when we invited Robert to Queensland to facilitate a workshop that I truly came to understand what it was I was seeking, as well as what I believe others are truly seeking.

When it was my turn to speak in the workshop, I found myself trapped in my memories of past experiences of how I was *supposed* to speak, what I was *supposed* to say. I was completely lost in all my programming and my fears around what people would think, that they wouldn't understand me, that they wouldn't want to hear what I have to say. So many judgments filled my head, I could barely talk: *I can't talk right, what if I am wrong* … the list went on almost endlessly. However, with each talk I gave, and with Robert's guidance and encouragement, I began to lift this burden of self-suppression. Then, a kind of miracle happened!

For the first time in my life, I heard *myself*, the me that lived hiding behind all the masks and under all the covers! I cried tears of joy and sadness at this discovery; and this recollection still brings tears to my eyes as I capture that moment.

I had the feeling of true freedom to express myself, a new kind of wholeness in allowing *me* to come forward and share my heartfelt thoughts and feelings, authentically, with arms wide open and vulnerable to a small group of people who were truly listening.

In a flash, I had come to realize what it meant to *bring out* and that "I am the message!" We are *all* the message! What had been lost within me was my own true authentic message, my true self — lost in everything I had been saying because I was supposed to say this, or not supposed to say that, caught up in what I thought others wanted me to say or were willing to hear.

I had finally broken through that impenetrable door that had locked me out of my own self, my true and authentic self. Robert talks about telling the truth. How simple is that?! Just speak from your heart. This simple formula for expressing our truth is what I found the courage to do: to *bring out* my true self in full view of others, without fear of rejection or judgment. What came through me, to my delight, was life itself in full expression!

What happens when we tell the truth, when we let our shining light out for all to see, when we truly embrace our own uniqueness, gifts, and creativity? For me, the world became brighter. The judgments — from myself and others — which I had believed to be so real and fearful could no longer intimidate me or hurt me. They had lost their status! Robert warned us in the course that we would always be judged by others, whether positive or negative, but that those judgments were just another person's truth, their opinion, and not the Gospel Truth. He said, "We are each a wave of opinion living in a sea of speculation!"

I learned to just joyfully say "Thank you for your opinion" to *any* judgment. I would no longer collapse and fall silent, or say things that were not true for me, just to win the approval and acceptance of others. I would stand in *my* truth and continue to listen inside myself and then speak out loud what came to me from this amazing creative force that lives within me, and you, that we can call self-expression.

In childcare development, when a child expresses for the first time on paper with a pencil, we say, "Today I expressed myself in the world. Today I left my mark on the world." Are we not doing that from the moment we are born? Are we not expressing ourselves and leaving our mark in and on the world with each word? When we pass away from this life, is it not how we lived, how we expressed the life force, that people remember? Isn't our living and our legacy how truly and authentically we speak, how we show up in life?

To me this is the single most important principle, the foundation, of all that we are and can aspire to become — that we know we can express ourselves and communicate authentically, honestly, and openly to and for the world, inviting confidence and love and joy in ways that truly connect us to others in our daily interactions. The key message that came from more than 100 inner child sessions was, "I just want to love and feel loved." This is, it seems to me, the desire to truly communicate this expression of our inner truth without fear, in intimate connection with others.

The workshop gently opened a personal knowing within me that has now come forward in my life, affecting change within myself and in all areas of my life — in my relationships, my work, my social life — that have been truly joyful uplifting and freeing. I have dreamed about this as a way of living all my life, and here it is!

By being *me*, openly and honestly, without fear of being a tall poppy (as we say here in Australia), I have had more people open themselves to me in a way where we both feel a connectedness that is based on wanting to share, with respect, our truth. It's very organic; it's as if when one person begins to tell the truth, others can't wait to jump in! I have experienced greater intimacy in my relationships, even with telemarketers! In being open to give and receive true communication, I have received more assistance and better service from people who are "just doing their job." What I am finding is that when we are willing to speak from our heart — openly, honestly, and with vulnerability — we are able to influence all aspects of our lives, often in surprising ways.

I have felt the difference as a mother, a wife, a businessperson, a workshop facilitator, an Inner Child practitioner, a friend, a daughter, a customer, a marketer. I get that while I have many roles in life, it is the authenticity of my being present and speaking from the heart that prevents me from being swallowed by the roles and their demands, and keeps me in front of, not behind, the masks. In this way I am finding out how to bring the joy of my self in to all that I do, just by being willing to speak my heart!

I am no longer afraid of standing out, of being a tall poppy. In fact, I want to be the tallest poppy in the field! (But so can you, there is room enough for all of us to be as tall as we want!) I truly invite you to stand here with me where we can experience our greatness together, no longer sharing our weakness and fears of standing out; stand with me to shout out loud, to live out loud: *I am here and this is my truth!*

Commentary

"When you find your voice, your life takes on grace."
M. Night Shyamalan

Sherrie refers to the "tall poppy syndrome," a peculiarly Australian idea that I had never heard of before moving here from the United States in 2005. The tall poppy syndrome is a topic that comes up in every one of my workshops here in Australia. It is a fire-walk that many have to take in order to break the hold of this socialization, their learned reticence to stand up, stick out, and speak brilliantly, powerfully, passionately, authentically! I may have first heard of this syndrome in Australia, but strands and strains of it exist everywhere throughout the world, in all cultures and societies.

My first direct experience of this tall poppy notion came one morning in a workshop I was leading. I wondered aloud why a few of the participants danced so delicately around an issue they wanted to discuss. They demurred, suggested, inferred. They did everything but speak plainly. I encouraged them to speak more boldly and directly. In our subsequent conversation, they said they had learned to not be bold or direct. They said that it wasn't right to speak out too loudly. They didn't want to stick out, or stand above the others. They told me about the tall poppy syndrome, which I've come to understand as a kind of cultural suppression of creative self-expression.

When I asked one of my Australian friends to give me her definition of the tall poppy syndrome, she said, "Let's not get too high and mighty, let's not get too carried away with ourself. We don't want anyone getting too full of their own talent or accomplishment. If they do, why we'll just cut them down to size. We'll have no tall poppies in our fields!"

Another said, "Australians are carrying a national consciousness of unworthiness, stemming from our roots as a convict colony. When one of us tries to move into the bigger world, to dream a bigger vision, we briefly project all of our personal unmet ambitions onto him. When it turns out he is human and experiences a moment of failure, or is in our eyes somehow not good enough or undeserving, we pull him down justifying our own choice not to have at least tried to expand our horizons. Just like the elephants tied to the chains who don't realize they are bigger than the chains, we are re-creating our convict history via our tall poppy syndrome, believing ourselves to be prisoners simultaneously worshipping, fearing, and resenting the ones who [illegible]ee."

And another friend talked about the "cultural cringe, a peculiarly Aussie malaise, a leveling attitude that seeks to keep people chained to mediocrity: in thinking and doing and dreaming big dreams — but most of all, in speaking. We're just not supposed to speak up. That would be big-noting and arrogant. That's for the Americans."

I am not speaking against modesty, nor am I speaking on behalf of wild arrogance or the unwarranted elevation of others as in the vulgar worship of "celebrities," one of the United States' cultural pathologies. I am talking about our right to own our own voice and vision, about our right to fully express our own *aliveness* as only we can. To do so is not arrogant or self-centered, but natural.

I think of how natural it is for children throughout the world to exult in discovering their creative and expressive powers! Once we can make a sound, we start gurgling, humming, singing, crying, wailing — wow, look, we can make sounds! Once we can crawl, and then walk and skip, you can't keep us penned in! And then, we can draw! We can create with color, with pencils, pens, crayons, paint — on everything! And then, to the dismay of all grown-ups, we realize we can make music by banging with *this* on *that*! The poet Derek Walcott surely wrote this line for children in the throes of discovery: *Feast on your life!*

Expressing ourself in uniquely creative ways is natural. It is the feast prepared for us at the moment we were created. And it is also natural to want to be appreciated and recognized for our creative expressions, for they represent our very essence of being! Look at the gleam and glow of any child as they rush to show a parent or teacher their picture — all excitement, joy, and pride! The only, *I repeat: the only*, appropriate response is overwhelming appreciation and encouragement. If we in any way ignore, disparage, or dismiss their work, we do the same to them; we will have hurt and wounded, perhaps fatally, their self-image and self-esteem, their enthusiasm and joy, their confidence and courage.

Since I have always been interested in the transformative power and inspirational potential of public speaking, I began to extrapolate this tendency to underachieve. If people were guarding against authentic self-expression and self-censoring heartfelt sentiments, if people were aiming for the lowest common denominator, if people were afraid to be vulnerable and transparent, to connect intimately with others ... what happens to people's soul? How would this cultural leveling mechanism restrict and repress a person's urge to rise above mediocrity?

What happens?

What happens when you begin to speak in unauthorized, powerful, poetic, passionate ways? What happens when your speaking sets you apart, because you are clear, confident, compelling? What happens when you begin to speak the unspeakable, which rocks the status quo, or which gives shape and texture to new possibilities, new freedoms, new solutions? What happens when you speak dreams and visions from other levels of consciousness, from other dimensions of being? What happens if you question a public official's rhetoric?

Hey, that's enough!! Stop right there! Who do you think you are to say such things? You have gone far enough. Now be quiet, mister, or you are going to find yourself in a world of trouble.

In a Sydney workshop, one woman told of standing in front of her class, I guess she was about seven years old, to show her picture. Everyone had been told to draw snowflakes. This woman proudly showed a picture of multi-colored snowflakes, not a single one was white! How original! How imaginative! How colorful!

Oops, no. The teacher had apparently lost too many important brain cells. What happened was that the teacher raced forward, grabbed the picture, held it aloft and began almost screaming: "Look at this! Children, look at this! This is *wrong*! Snowflakes are *white*. Everyone knows that! Have you ever seen colored snowflakes?! *No!* Now go back to your seat and do this over, and do it *right.*"

In the midst of this public shaming, this poor little girl just then and there decided for all time: *I am not good enough. I cannot draw. I am stupid. I will never again dream, imagine, or do anything different.*

These self-limiting decisions in the face of life events are the beginning of what I call diminished capacity, which is the major, if not singular, cause underlying our inability to lead truly authentic, happy, creative lives of intimacy and originality. Once we shut down and close off, we are cut off from the very life-force we need to be whole, to be powerful, to be passionate, to be productive, to be successful in whatever way we want.

The tall poppy syndrome, especially as it pertains to speaking, is not proprietary to Australia. It is universal. Every society and each culture has sought to regulate speaking with bribes and intimidations. We all have to learn to speak our truth from the depths of our being, heart to heart and eye to eye. We all have to transform diminished capacity into ferocious and fearless speaking and truth-telling. This is where and how we connect with our life-force, how we inspire ourselves to dream big dreams, to take on big, foolish projects like Noah, to bring forth fire, and to learn to love the Earth.
It is in this free flowing authenticity of our creative and expressive impulses that the inner and outer become one and whole, that we discover our path in

life, that we actualize our deepest longings, and find our place in the world.

Sherrie and I have become friends. She tells me — via text, email, or phone — of her growing fondness for speaking her truth, of living out loud. She tells me of her speaking adventures and insights, which are many! She is a powerhouse, a real force. I love how she brings forth her voice and passion from deep inside herself, as if a giant wild wave were coming from the sea to swamp mediocrity and smallness, to wash over the complacent cities of our timid living.

The Upward Spiral

Caroline Power

I met Robert last year when Ida Lyall hosted an afternoon in which he gave a presentation to a small group of people in Carnegie. The topic for the session was Silence and I recall Robert discussing how important it is in our day-to-day lives. After the presentation my friend Mary introduced me to Robert and also told me about Robert's public speaking course that she had completed and just loved.

I remember feeling somewhat intimidated to meet the presenter but also intrigued that this guy from America was impressing people who I trusted. What I did not understand was how public speaking could possibly be a "spiritual" practice. I knew that I wanted to do the course but public speaking is just not my thing so I put it off for a few months. During that time, however, I often thought about the course and felt somewhat intrigued. I often looked at Robert's website and read testimonials of participants who raved about the course.

Several months later I sent Robert an email. I told him that I was terrified but that another part of me really wanted to do the course. At the time, the fear was debilitating. I guess that on some level I knew that I would have to put myself on the line. I would have to risk having people watch me and deal with my misconceptions of other people's judgments. I guess that I was almost hoping he would tell me that the course was not for someone so scared or that it was already fully booked. Robert responded almost immediately. He said that he had remembered meeting me and that I should get ready to get over the fear because he had added my name for the next course. And he said not to worry about the deposit, just pay on the day. Oh shit!!! He took away all the obstacles!

On the first morning of the course I drove to Robert's place absolutely terrified. I was grateful that Robert's opening went for a while but the terror did not subside. When my turn arrived to stand in front of the room and introduce myself, I contemplated leaving but I just could not give in like that. So I sat in the chair and quite honestly told the group what was in my heart: "I really don't want to be here." I tried to make a quick exit from the spotlight only to have Robert ask me to remain seated and allow others to see me. How does this guy know my weaknesses, he had only known me for a few hours? I have spent so many years of my life trying not to be noticed and only an hour or so into the course Robert has coaxed me to stop running from my self

-imposed terror and just sit and be seen. I felt very uneasy.

By the second day of the course and after several small presentations, I decided that I would share with the group my experience of yoga. Until that point I had never really stopped to consider why I do yoga or what it means to me. From somewhere other than my conscious mind I described yoga as a tool that I use to find refuge from my ever-present, ever-battering mind. Somewhere in the midst of that short talk, I found that place that I had experienced in yoga. It was the most awesome feeling. It was also quite daunting.

By the end of the course I was in awe of this public speaking workshop and Robert's ability to guide people to where they needed to go. I was also amazed by the group dynamics. That group of people, who were complete strangers just two days earlier, had become a very compassionate and open community, giving and receiving love and support.

I left the course committed to my on-going practice of my speaking with confidence and excited by the possibilities which I thought would open for me. Robert emailed me a week or so after the first course and invited me to be his guest at the next course to continue facing down my fears of public speaking. I didn't hesitate to accept.

I entered the second course with less apprehension than the first but the challenges of being present and being seen were still there. Each time that I made my way to the front of the room my inner self-doubt would amplify and I would stand almost paralyzed by the negativity in my mind. Each time, though, I would become a little more confident and dare to expose just a little more of myself. Again I left Robert's course enthused and determined to use these new skills. Still, I found that after a month or so I had slipped back into my old ways.

Four months after completing the second course I traveled to India to practice yoga. I traveled alone and was more than ready by day two to pack up and leave but just like when I wanted to leave Robert's first course, this time, too, I knew that I could not give in to my fears. Even after making that decision to stay in India, I was haunted by my fears; but I also knew from Robert's workshop that meeting your fears and moving through them is the only way to overcome them and become free.

I spent a few days in a timid daze carefully moving about the town where I was going to live for the next month. I also started what would be my first commitment to a daily yoga practice. As I attended classes I made friends with other students and the fears I experienced in the first couple of days subsided.

During my month in India I spent a lot of time thinking about

Robert's workshop and realized that it is so much more than public speaking or communication. It is a lesson in consciousness and it is so encompassing. Communication is a tool that is used time and time again every day and the skill to do so is not often taught. More importantly to me was the realization that my ways of communication are habitual, mostly unconscious, and have been ingrained in me from early infancy. Every interaction that I have now is an opportunity for practice and an opportunity to interact in a new way, a way without burdens of the past. So there I was half way across the world practicing yoga without any comprehension as to why when I realized that yoga and Speak Truthfully are so, so similar. The beauty of Speak Truthfully is that you don't need a mat or a class to practice and you are not limited to practice only during the times that you are on your mat. Rather, Speak Truthfully is an ongoing practice that is relevant wherever you are, whatever you are doing.

When I returned from India I signed up for another of Robert's workshops. Even though it was the third time that I had taken the course it felt like I was taking it for the first time. The difference between the first two courses and the third was that I was far less terrified of standing before an audience and being noticed. The third course also confirmed for me that it is a practice that gets easier the more that you do it. And just like yoga, any excuse that may hold you back from starting or practicing is the very thing that is so valuable in overcoming. The most poignant thing that I took away from the course this third time was how masterful you become when you are present. I sat in awe of Robert as he spoke with absolute precision, telling a story or imparting information. For two days I was in total awe of his mastery in speaking. I am yearning for those skills, to be able to speak with precision, spontaneity, and wit — and to have fun doing it!

It is now nine months since I first completed Robert's workshop. I have just begun the trip of my life, living in New York City for the next few months. I have the luxury to be able to practice yoga daily and I am also blessed to have had Robert share his knowledge with me. It has only been in the past day or two that I have really realized that yoga does take me to the place beyond my battering mind. Yoga creates a space for the truth in me to reveal itself and for me to have fun in the world, without feeling oppressed by my negativity and self-doubt.

It also keeps me on an upward spiral of dedication and commitment to my person growth. So while I am off my mat I can still be practicing what I love so much when I am on my mat.

Commentary

"Yoga is stilling the modifications of mind."
Patanjali

When I think of Caroline, I smile and my heart expands. She is truly an amazing young woman. Her courage and determination are like mountains with no summits, they are so huge. For good reason is her last name Power.

I have led personal growth workshops for 25 years. I have had to learn how to let people be in their process, experiencing what is theirs to experience, without being manipulated by their thoughts and emotions. Empathy, I learned, is different from sympathy. Despite my years of experience, Caroline certainly tempted me to interfere in her process, to intrude on the opportunity she was giving herself to move beyond her fear. I almost ruined her magnificent heroine's journey, because I almost couldn't bear to witness her terror!

In her first talk in her first workshop, she sat in a chair looking like she was going to die right then and there. She was gripping the sides of the chair so tightly, her hands and wrists became white as eggshells. Caroline will never know (until she reads this) how close I came to saying, "Caroline, it's OK. You don't have to. Really. You can leave. It's OK. You can go home. Please." But she was more warrior than I was, and she sat in that chair, then stood, time after time, day after day, course after course. I think it was in her third course that she waltzed up to the front of the room, with a bright and fearless smile, and proceeded to give a completely impromptu talk lasting about 8 minutes. From where she started, that is farther than light travels in 10 years at a speed of 186,000 miles per second! As if that weren't gorgeous enough, a few weeks ago I got an email from her, I think she was in India, asking about becoming a Speak Truthfully facilitator! I love that!

I love the way Caroline draws comparisons between yoga and public speaking. She writes, "Yoga creates a space for the truth in me to reveal itself and for me to have fun in the world, without feeling oppressed by my negativity and self-doubt." She observes, in yoga and speaking, how we become masterful when we become present. In reading her words, I realized why I love public speaking so much, because more than anything else, it creates a space for the truth in me to reveal itself and for me to have fun in the world, without feeling oppressed by my negativity and self-doubt! Thank you, Caroline!

I teach five simple speaking practices that help us become present and thus, like the practice of yogic postures, stable within our truth and steady in our authentic connection to self and others. These five simple practices help put the YOU in your speaking. I've field-tested these for 20 years. They work. I introduce these to people in workshops and they find their speaking becomes much more authentic, their presence more compelling — immediately. It's not necessary to "do" these in some order. Rather, become aware of them, work with them, and install them into your mental, emotional, and physical memory so they become automatic.

Breathe: In a recent workshop, I asked a woman to comment on her talk, after watching it in playback. She said, "I can see that I forgot to breathe!" Mercifully, it was only a two-minute talk! I suggested to her that she remember to breathe in her talks, otherwise she'd run into some real trouble with those longer ones.

An Aikido teacher friend of mine used to say: "Breathing: once in the morning isn't enough!" Almost everyone I know loses awareness of their breathing when they are speaking. I do not know of a better, faster, or more powerful means of becoming present than to be aware that you are breathing. Before you start speaking, take a few slow, deep breaths. Return to awareness of your breathing throughout your speaking because it helps you to stay connected with yourself and your audience. It settles your mind. It calms your nerves. It connects you to now. Breathing deeply also gives depth of tone to your voice.

Ground: One of the elements of our speaking instrument is our body. If you were ever fortunate enough to see the late Marcel Marceau, the insanely talented mime artist, you'll know how important your body is. Our speaking, even if our words are stunning and heavenly, is still a physical act. In order to establish a firm physical posture and presence, feel your feet on the ground and then visualize a root growing from your feet into the center of the Earth. This will help you stay connected to your body, the audience, and the environment. Grounding doesn't prevent you from moving around; it will enable you to move with energy and awareness. This recognition of your body will help you speak with your whole being, not just your mouth.

Gather: Before speaking, take as much time as you need to become fully present in front of your audience. Allow the audience to see you, and become completely comfortable being seen. Gather your focus, your thoughts, your energy. Gather your equilibrium and poise. Gather the whole audience into your awareness. Speak when, not before, you are ready. I never begin speaking — whether in a workshop, individual or group coaching session, or keynote — until I have gathered myself, until I am fully present within myself and connected to the audience. This principle, Gather, makes a huge difference for people right away.

I can't believe how many speakers begin speaking too quickly. You can see that they are not settled in themselves, they have not established an energetic connection with the audience, they are not relating in real-time to what's present in the room, to what's going on. They just turn and start speaking. No. Don't do that. Never do that. Always Gather. It may only take a second or two, it may take a minute. I've sometimes used five or more minutes. The principle is to become present and aware before you begin. Or, to say that better, Gather should always be the beginning.

Connect: Connection comes before communication. If there is no connection between speaker and audience, there is no communication, there is only broadcasting. We do not want to stand in front of people and broadcast some words in their general direction. That is not public speaking. Please don't do that. Connection is part intentional, part physical, and part energetic. It is the essence of "intimacy with self and vulnerability with others." Take some time to really see your audience, feel them, link up with them. Let them do the same. Let them really see you. Your speaking should go from inside you to inside them, and you've got to create that link, that connection, through which your words and feelings and meanings can flow. Before speaking, and throughout your speaking, feel this connection.

Contact: The audience is your friend. They want to experience you, even more than what you are saying. Eye contact is an essential physical component of connection. Take the time to make eye contact with members of the audience, smile, extend yourself to them as you would greet your favorite friend. Don't look over them, through them, or around them. Look at one person, and then another, and then another. Always look at a particular person, make eye contact in a natural way. Smile. Open. Extend. Receive. Connect. I can't speak unless I am looking at someone; I need to have my eyeballs on someone's eyeballs, or I immediately lose the life of my speaking, which is based on connection. If I'm not looking at someone, who the hell am I connecting with, the ceiling?

Synchronicity

Hermine Zielinski

Yes, I was the person who became literally "unconscious" when I was in front of people. Shaking, throwing up (before speaking or afterwards, thankfully never during), not sleeping for days before any kind of a talk in front of others, could never get my words out clearly. I even almost quit a very good job because they told me I had to make a presentation to about 50 people. (And that presentation didn't go well, so it helped me build up my story of how I was a really BAD speaker.) For a manager who has to address groups on a regular basis, this was not a happy state of affairs!

I did a regular public speaking course which helped. It allowed me to practice getting up and talking in front of people and gave me some tools to observe what I was doing so I could give better speeches (providing I remained conscious enough to use them!). After the course I thought I'd better put what I had learned into practice, so I gave a couple of presentations and volunteered to speak in front of people wherever I could. I did get better; however, I still wasn't friends with my nerves! I noticed that when I was very relaxed and didn't care about the outcome of the speech or was in a familiar environment I was fine: not only fine, but I was getting compliments on my natural ability as a speaker. When I did care about the speech, back came the shakes, my inability to read notes, and pockets of time I had no memory of, etc. This paradox, as you can imagine, was baffling to me.

Call it chance, coincidence, whatever, but two days after I had made that definite decision to quit my job, I received an email advertising Speak Truthfully. I looked up Robert's website and knew this would be a good follow-up to the initial public speaking course I had done, so I signed up.

I wasn't sure what to expect. I knew it was going to be different, but I had no idea how much. Throughout the weekend Robert helped me discover many things, and other realizations continued to arise well after the course.

Quite often during the course we were asked to speak about a subject given to us only moments before. We had no time to prepare or rehearse. I remember standing up and having no idea of what I would say — and I let this panic me. When the panic set in, it was consuming: I got red in the face, the shakes came, and my thoughts froze.

Here was the paradox again. When I was in conversation with friends or colleagues in a one-on-one or small group, I was fine. I always found words and didn't feel uncomfortable. So why was it different when I spoke to an unknown group or large crowd? I was seeing the audience as one thing: a big, scary, multi-headed monster. (And I could not bring myself to trust that the words would come while I was imagining that!) One of the things Robert focused on that helped with this was saying that even with an audience of many, you are only communicating with one person at a time. When I focused on speaking to one person at a time, and not on the entire multi-headed monster, the scariness of the "group" disappeared and it felt like I was having a one-on-one conversation. The nerves subsided, I relaxed, and the words came, usually only a moment before they were spoken but a moment is enough. My memory wouldn't hold much more than that anyway!

Allowing myself to be vulnerable, for others to see me, was scary. Standing up there in front of others with all of them looking at *me* — I felt see-through and extremely open to judgment and criticism. The self-confidence I had when in familiar surroundings disappeared. However, as Robert said, great public speaking requires "intimacy with self and vulnerability with others," his formula for authentic connection. Through various exercises he encouraged us to be comfortable being up there, allowing ourselves to be seen and judged. After all, people will have an opinion about you, positive or negative. He suggested we get used to that, and understand that judgment was just people's opinions. After a while my nerves started to settle and I felt more secure (my knees even stopped shaking at one point!). When I *allowed* the judgment instead of trying to escape from it, that's when the real connection with the audience happened. If I blocked any part of me, if I tried to hide from the audience, then I was also blocking the connection I could have with them. Open to send, open to receive. I didn't want to be judged but as Robert pointed out, it's not something you can do anything about. You will be judged, get used to it! I also think if I'm speaking *my* truth, no one else can fully know what that is, so their judgment shouldn't really make me doubt my truth. I still notice other people's judgment, but it kind of flows over me now rather than making me cringe.

One of the major developments from the weekend came on Saturday night, after the first day of the two-day workshop. I woke up in the middle of the night and couldn't sleep; my mind was racing from everything that had happened on the first day. I realized that I was still living in one of my many stories. In the past, I have been quiet, and somewhat reserved when communicating with others. Yet every now and again a burst of energy would force its way out that usually resulted in some outlandish behavior or saying something that other people considered quite out of character. Dressing extravagantly or being the life of a party after a few drinks were a couple of the tamer manifestations of this bursting energy! These were certainly not planned and I felt somewhat out of control when they happened. It was like something in me was trying to escape. I would often be embarrassed by these behaviors, sometimes asking myself whether I was perhaps unstable, manic, or didn't know where my boundaries were. I was unsure of this energy, as I thought it was bad and scared me with what it might mean or bring. When I explored this further what I discovered was a layering of repressions based on ideals of society, family and friends, and protective behavior patterns from my own experiences. Really it was all based on a story I was living. I was repressing the energy that would build within me, and instead of allowing it to flow through me and show itself freely, I was holding it in, and then when it overloaded it would burst out on its own.

To communicate my own truth I had first to acknowledge myself as I was, no pretending, no story. This meant recognizing and letting go of these repressions and ideals as they arose. That night I let go of my story of why I shouldn't be comfortable with who I really was, and gave myself permission to live out loud. I then had to allow my truth to be communicated using my own unique creative expression, letting go of the tendency to repress what wants to come out, however it wishes to do this.

There was a disconnect between what I was thinking and feeling and what I was communicating to others. Why? To fit in, not offend anyone, not appear too different, to avoid judgment. I did not want this to continue so I began to let the energy flow freely and show itself however and whenever it wants to. This wasn't an instant process and took effort and the choice to observe my own behavior and thoughts, and gently guide myself back when I'm going astray. What has happened is the disconnect from who I really am and what I display to others is dissolving. What's left? Just me and my voice. Like riding the horse or flying the glider, I feel in sync with me.

Now, how do I summarize the weekend? Freeing? Revealing? Certainly amazing!

When I watched the video of my last talk, it was very surreal. It was like watching someone else. It took me a few days to let it sink in that it was me and I was capable of really connecting with the audience and speaking from the heart. It wasn't perfect but I saw I had tapped into being able to realize and speak my own truth, so the biggest step was taken. From here, it is a matter of exploring, practicing, and refining.

Since the workshop all my communications have been more authentic and real, not just at work but with friends and family. I have spoken in front of groups a few times and, yes, I do remember most of them! I won't say the nerves are gone but I believe they are becoming my friend. I believe everyone has it in them to speak from the heart with passion and power. Speak

Truthfully is the best vehicle I've experienced to discover how to allow myself to do that.

Gradually, as everything comes together and becomes clearer, this has become more than a way of speaking but a way of living. My life has taken on a sense of flow or synchronicity that really is quite magical.

Commentary

"Do not go where the path may lead,
go instead where there is no path and leave a trail."
Ralph Waldo Emerson

Hermine is physically imposing, almost six feet tall, and everything about her seems powerful and strong, including her spirit. How ironic, then, that she was one of those people who "literally goes unconscious" when talking in front of people she doesn't know! In those moments, what happens to her wild spirit and strength, and where do the horses and eagles go? Hermine knows the answer, and illuminates it brilliantly: *layering of repressions based on ideals of society, family, and friends, and protective behavior patterns.*

Layering of repressions and *protective behavior patterns* is a true account of what happens in our life. We start out with full access to our wild and free nature. We start out in life friends with horses and eagles, with powerful natural forces. But along the way, we are told that these friends are not appropriate, they are too unpredictable, too strong for polite society. So, we begin to layer repressions, in order to fit with the ideals and expectations of society, family, and friends.

In one of her talks during the workshop, Hermine mentioned how she was a quiet child, hardly ever speaking until, one day, she was put on a horse, and there, on that powerful, muscular animal, she immediately began chattering nonstop. There, on that horse, she connected with her spirit, with her courage and confidence, with her life-force. The horse gave her a transmission of spirit!

But the layers of repression kept that wild and natural energy locked inside when she wasn't on the horse. But Hermine knew that great and powerful energy cannot remain there; it is meant to break out and gallop, or fly! As long as we are saddled with doubt and suspicion, the energy comes out in weird ways, as she mentions. That energy must come out, even if it has to break out in sudden bursts and frighten everyone who is near the bursting.

When we reclaim our wild nature, our original power and beauty of self-expression, when we are able to accept ourself and our truth, when we are able to stand before others and say, *Here I am* — then we free that energy from the layers of repression to come out in organic and graceful ways.

That is what Hermine did in her final talk of the workshop. She told the story of the horse that she felt would take her to World Cup Showjumping and of how the horse contracted a tumor, which ended her dream. I don't think it was easy to tell that story; one can guess at all the emotions that would run along with it.

In telling that story, Hermine became completely transparent, her feelings fully on display. Then and there, her authentic spirit came out; nothing was in the way. She connected with people, looking one then another straight in the eye, opening herself for us to see the depth of her feeling. She showed and said, in that moment, *I am no longer going to hide. I am not going to live beneath these layers of repression. I am going to let my horses gallop, my eagles fly, my spirit soar. I am going to show you who I am.*

Hermine demonstrates the potential of public speaking to transform even a lifetime of habit, of layered repression. Maybe in the same way she senses thermals in the high-above places she soars in, she sensed her own inhibitions standing in front of us; but she also sensed the gathering storm clouds of her wild energy, and she chose her freedom. It was a beautiful moment of revelation, of uncovering, of transformation, of vulnerability. Everyone will remember that.

Creating a Culture of Conscious Communication

Lou Bacher

In April 2009 I accompanied my partner to a weekend workshop on speaking truthfully that was being facilitated by Robert. I went along to give her the moral support I thought she needed as she was growing a new business and Pauline wanted to become a more confident speaker. I didn't require any development as I had been at the pointy end of leading business for 25 years and knew how to speak — or so I thought.

Not long after the niceties of a welcome and participants introductions, Robert set the class a task to stand up and speak impromptu for a couple of minutes each. He said that he wanted to get a feel for how we showed up in our speaking. As he announced this first assignment, my mind catapulted me into the abyss of fear, doubt, and self-consciousness. How dare he, I thought: no preparation time, no research time — how does he expect me to be at my best as a presenter if he didn't give me the time to prepare my content and rehearse my delivery!

My turn came around quicker than I wanted. As I stood up I was gripped with the fear of making a fool of myself. I wrestled with my "not good enough demons" as I faced the audience and spoke. Well, you can guess how well my talk landed what with all that noise going on in my head. I sat down after what seemed like an eternity to hear Robert's assessment of how I was speaking. He asked me just two questions. Were you present and fully aware while you were speaking? Who exactly were you speaking to? Something clicked inside me right then.

Throughout the two days, as Robert spoke and as we spoke, that click kept recurring. By the end of the two-day workshop, I had really understood and integrated Robert's basic premise in speaking, that it's all about credibility. We have to be truthful enough, present enough, visible enough, intimate enough with our audience for them to believe us, which is different than believing the information we are giving out. I had always assumed that people were looking solely at the content of my presentations. Robert was saying something entirely different. He said people get to our content through us, through the speaker. YOU are the message, he says over and over. He taught us that to be credible and believable, to be a truly great speaker, we need to speak truthfully with comfort, confidence, authenticity, shakti (energy, life force), and silence. Each of these terms has precise meanings and implications in his program.

For the first time in my life I had some real-time awareness of how I was speaking and what I was saying, while I was saying it — and so the magic started to happen with my speaking. I gained access to my authenticity. I began to be vulnerable in front of people, and I began to truly connect with people in my audiences.

I couldn't help but think of how valuable this would be in my company. In the business I was running I had spent the previous eight months recruiting a new management team for the company. As the managing director, I asked Robert to develop and conduct a program that was focused on how we were speaking to our customers and to our people. I knew that what I had learned in the public workshop would be as powerful in business. In my role as MD, I knew that credibility was essential to my leadership role. I knew that our managers and our sales team needed to same understanding of how to be truly credible, not because of their positional standing in the company or because of our sales pitch, but because of their personal believability. We needed to create a communication culture in which these principles would be the baseline and standard.

The idea behind this program was that since all performance and productivity are based on communication, then why don't we have a clear set of communication principles, or standards, that would give us the best chance of success? With this in mind, we set in motion the means to transform our culture to one of conscious communication standards and customer care principles — all based on the Speak Truthfully philosophy.

Robert facilitated a meeting with key stakeholders. What resulted was a set of communication principles that everyone in the company agreed to embrace and embody. They became cornerstone of how the company engaged with customers and employees. It was based on Integrity, transparency, and self-awareness. It was based on speaking truthfully.

We defined the communication principles in terms of behaviors. We wanted to be sure people knew that principles had to be acted out, they had to show up in our face-to-face encounters with each other.

What I noticed after Robert's program, and it happened very quickly, was a new level of cohesion in how everyone went about their work. The team trusted each other's capabilities, and they developed the willingness to openly share their ideas.

About a year after these programs, encouraged and supported by Robert, I decided to leave my position and, in fact, say good-bye to my corporate leadership career. For what? To teach what I have learned over the years, of course. I have founded Adaptive Thinking, a coaching and consulting firm offering people in the public, private, and business sectors a variety of programs. There is a common thread to all my offerings: the power and joy of authenticity in living, working, and speaking. Speaking truthfully.

Commentary

In formation, flying towards each other at 500 miles per hour;
1600 hundred feet per second,
with wingtips passing at maybe 4 feet; if each pilot is off by one second
it would displace their crossing point by 4 city blocks.
Blue Angels Navy Flight Demonstration Team

Lou's essay gives me a chance to touch on the organizational rather than the personal dimension of speaking truthfully.

Lou writes, "The idea behind this program was that since all performance and productivity are based on communication, then why don't we have a clear set of communication principles, or standards, that would give us the best chance of success?" Indeed, why not?

I have consulted to a number of organizations large and small; corporate, non-profit, academic, and public sector. My areas of consulting are leadership and communication, and I work primarily with senior managers and above. At this executive level, the focus is usually on performance, productivity, vision, values, and, of course, the financial bottom line.

In every organization I've worked in, executives strive to solicit high performance and outstanding productivity from their teams. These twin preoccupations are a function of how well people communicate. This is just as true up and down the ladder, left to right, and all around. Not just how well, but how truthfully people communicate.

The dream culture is one in which every employee contributes their best self and abilities every day, is fully engaged in their work, meets problems creatively, communicates in an open and honest manner, is loyal and committed. You might think people do this because they are professionals, have skills, and are paid on time. If you think this, you'd be wrong.

This kind of culture has to be carefully constructed, nurtured, and maintained. In my view, the single most important element of building this kind of culture is truthful speaking. This idea must be clearly defined, modeled, expected, inspected, acknowledged, and rewarded.

This is the program I did with Lou's company. It works. People do want to bring their best to work, they do want to flourish and thrive and create. But in order to do those things, they have to feel safe to tell the truth. As we know, that is often very risky in corporate cultures. There are so many ways in which people are afraid of truth-telling, from humiliation to reprisals.

Powerful egos and hard-driving managers don't always want people to tell the truth, unless it is theirs.

Organizations that do not encourage and support authentic communication suppress the very spirit and energy with which people work. If you aren't safe to speak your truth, you will collapse inside and work with half a heart and no real enthusiasm. People have to feel safe first. This is part of the cultural foundation of conscious communication principles — safety. It has to be created. People have to feel it. That safety for truth-telling can never be violated.

When people are not encouraged to speak truthfully or when they don't feel safe, they don't do it. Think of all the ways in which possibilities and opportunities are wasted because people withhold speaking truthfully, because they speak to be safe, instead of speaking to tell the truth. Stop reading for a moment, please, and reflect on what you know about this dynamic from your own experience. What is the upside of speaking truthfully, and what is the downside of not do so.

In my program, I like to show a short video clip of the Blue Angels Navy Flight Team. The footage is breathtaking. After I show the clip, I ask one question: How do these people speak to each other? And then we bring the conversation from the Blue Angels to the company.

We talk about what happens when people do speak truthfully, and in real time; and we speak about what happens when they don't. We look at current cultural and organizational impediments to truth-telling. We start to create a handful of communication principles, defined behaviorally. At some point they are ratified and rolled out. It's a much longer process than I have space to detail here.

I want to reinforce Lou's point: productivity and performance are a function of how well and how truthfully people communicate. Don't take for granted that people will, even though I believe most people want to.

Make truth-telling the foundation of a culture of conscious communication. Set people free.

Weekend Of Epiphanies

Dana Carr

Where to start, what to say? For me, I have had this belief for some time that I have a communication problem. I never had a problem talking; in fact, if I ever told people that I needed communication lessons they would think I was joking, as I talk quite a lot. However, I never felt I talked in a way that could be really heard. I never felt that people really heard me. I'm not saying it was their fault. I'm just saying. Hence my adventure in Speak Truthfully began with my sister telling me about this weekend workshop that she thought might help me communicate better.

The fears I faced going to the workshop were not fears of public speaking, as my sister did not even emphasize that part of it. In fact, I hardly knew it was a public speaking workshop! My fears had more to do with being seen as a failure by others and of being seen as slow to learn what I was being taught.

In spite of those fears, the weekend was a good time. I learned to see things from a different perspective and that what I think I say is not always what people hear. I also realized that a lot of things people said to me and about me were not gospel; they were just a lot of opinions. Just because they told me that's the way I should think, didn't make it right. I discovered no one is the boss of my thoughts. I always thought I was wrong, because everyone told me I was. Now I realize that it is all a matter of opinion.

After the course I felt very excited to try my Speak Truthfully attitudes and skills. I practiced at home to empty chairs, much to the entertainment of my children. Since the course I have used some of the philosophies in my everyday life, which has helped me to like myself a lot more since the day I walked into the workshop.

So, in closing, I can honestly say that the weekend helped me to discover a lot of amazing things about myself through love and laughter. What a great way to learn.

Robert asked me if I'd also share an email I sent him two weeks after the class. I thought it over, and here it is:

I wanted to let you know how you impacted me personally. The workshop was more about self-worth than public speaking, which I suppose intertwines, but it means so much more to me, because of your opinion that we are all fabulous just because we exist, and that we have a right to be whatever we choose. Thank you for seeing me, the person, not the failure I am so used to seeing myself as. You lifted my spirit and filled some little cracks in my heart that were created from other people's negative opinions. So, you being the best conversational male I know, I'll be wearing you in my heart forever. When I am 90, I'll be talking about a great man I paid to hear talk, because he was the best conversationalist in the world. And I'd pay to do it again. There is no price too high to find a loving, caring person like yourself. So don't ever dismiss this letter because you are not the boss of my thoughts!

You are one man who connected to my heart and spirit without judgment in just 16 hours, not an easy task. You're an awesome positive influence. On one serious note, and please feel free to use this letter as a testimonial for your workshops, as fun-loving as I am, I have had troubles like bulimia and been plagued by suicidal thoughts. Now those thoughts have changed to mere opinions, not truths. I can't express in words (as I cry writing this) how now, no matter how badly I think of myself, meeting you, and your just loving me for me as you did, and as you did for all of us, has helped me think how much I am worth. Just because you saw the real me which so many people refuse to see because they're just looking for possessions, job description, looks, wit, or the gift of gab.

I still sometimes feel worthless, but when I do, I think of you and how much you cared for all of us and that helps me to remember that there are people out there with great opinions. The next time I feel lifeless, I will be thinking of you, the person whose opinion meant the world to me. My life is everything because you saw me, acknowledged me, rewarded me, positively reinforced me, laughed with me, helped me to like me a little more. So if these words are not explanatory enough let me put it in plain English: when my heart hurts, I will remember you and your acceptance of my spirit and heart and I will not let my opinions of myself that "I am better off dead" lead me to thinking of suicide anymore.

I choose to change that opinion to one that what I say and do is funny, loving, and awesome. Something that small is so big, and meeting you just may have saved a mother, a wife, a daughter, a granddaughter, and a sister. I know I have gone on a bit but I had to explain how much it meant to me personally, physically, heartfelt; that meeting you put a patch on my heart to live more playfully, fully, lovingly. I know that I have a choice of thoughts and I choose what you think of me because it's better than my opinion of myself. So you did more than run a workshop. You saved a soul.

Thanks for just being you and for seeing the real me.

Commentary

"... everything flowers, from within, of self-blessing; though sometimes it is necessary to reteach a thing its loveliness ... and retell it in words and in touch it is lovely ..."
Galway Kinnell

Dana is a gutsy woman, strong and courageous. Prior to this workshop, she had never taken any kind of workshop, ever. So, when I asked her to stand up and introduce herself on the morning of the first day, she almost fell over in a faint. "I didn't know we'd have to talk in front of the group," she said.

"Dana, this is a public speaking workshop. What did you think, we'd mime our way through?"

Dana shot a look to Sherrie, who had "enrolled" her in the workshop with a cryptic comment, "Take it. You'll like it. It will be good for you." Even as the implications of the workshop were becoming apparent, Dana did not waver or falter. She did not step back. She stepped up, and forward.

As you can see from her essay and email, Dana had come to believe what some people had told her about herself. Dana came to the workshop with a pretty serious conviction that she was not smart, lovable, or accomplished. Her self-image was about as far from who I saw — who everyone saw, who she truly is — as one end of the universe is from the other.

In the workshop, I talk about the inevitable concerns and fears people have about being "wrong" in front of others, about being criticized and judged. This is one of the big issues around public speaking, isn't it? "What if I say something wrong? What if I say something that people think is silly, or stupid?"

I tell people to get used to it. On this planet, we judge each other, all the time. Incessantly. We can't stop. We can't walk past a mirror without doing it to ourselves: *God, I'm fat; my ass looks like a cruise ship! Look at my hair! Oh-oh, time for some nip and tuck there and there.*

The issue, I suggest, is not criticism and judgment, but whether or not we collapse and betray our truth and creative spirit in the face of it! Do we experience a sudden loss of cabin pressure in the face of people's thoughts about us?

One of the ways we elevate another person's opinion above our own is by placing that opinion on what I call a *vertical axis*. In other words, we create a hierarchical arrangement, whereby some people possess "truth." We use a variety of criteria to put people above us: title, social status, money, gender, religion, accomplishment, looks — even weight. (Never mind that some of the most successful people in the world, whose opinions we esteem, are psychopaths!) This hierarchical ordering of opinion is bound to create problems of self-doubt. If I believe that your thought is truer than mine, and if you think I'm crap, then I am.

I suggest to people, instead of building a vertical axis, build a horizontal axis, and put all of people's judgments on one plane, and reframe them as simply "opinions." My pet phrase on this topic is: *We are each a single wave of opinion living together in a sea swelling with speculation.*

Of course, I'm not demeaning experience or expertise. I want to be sure my dentist has graduated from dental school and knows her way around my mouth. I don't want anyone using pliers and brute force! In the same way, we are free to consider the thoughts and judgments of others, and take them on board if we want to. The point is this: we do not ever need to lose the cabin pressure of self-confidence in the face of other people's thoughts or opinions.

I ought to confess that underneath this extremely practical and pragmatic action of tilting the vertical axis on its side is a philosophical, even mystical, notion of existence. Here it is, my opinion: existence, creation, the cosmos, whatever the hell you want to call this incomprehensible mystery in which we live and of which we are a part, this *thing* is so huge, so vast, so complex and multi-dimensional that no one, no one, not even the latest guru *du jour*, not any scientist, saint, or sage, not any writer or artist, not any one who ever lived at any time in any place — no one knows nor can say the whole truth of the whole thing.

What do you know? What do you say? It may be less informed, less experienced, less accurate, less useful than another's opinion, but in terms of *your right to express yourself fully and without fear it is as valid as the next.* Why do we chase from one prophet to the next, begging for the inevitable disappointment because no one can give us what we are really looking for: authentic self-expression? I swear, Monty Python would have won an Oscar for their movie *Life of Brian* if they had entered it as a documentary.

I went to high school in Anaheim, California, in the backyard of Disneyland. Have you ever been to Disneyland? I haven't been in years and years, but I remember all these different worlds, like Tomorrowland and Frontierland, and ride after ride. For a little kid, or for a teenager "under the influence" it was quite something. Of course, we all had our favorite rides and some we hated and wouldn't go on no matter what. But even your favorite ride, the one you just knew was so much better than the others, that was just your opinion of one ride in a vast playground of dozens and scores and hundreds of rides and amusements. Life, existence, is like that. Everyone is on their favorite ride, shouting out their glee. That's just their opinion, their preference. And this is mine.

When we discuss this idea of a horizontal axis in the workshop, I talk about living a creative and expressive life, and how "right and wrong" and "good and bad" are too small a context in which to live. Our lives as expressive beings need a bigger context, a bigger frame of reference, one that asks us to evaluate how authentic and how truthful we are being. I tell people that to express your truth, to tell the simple story of "this is what I think, this is what I feel, this is what I want, and this is what I don't want" cannot exist in a right-wrong, good-bad polarity.

This philosophy is what leads me to say to people in my workshops, "I'm not trying to be right, and I'm not afraid of being wrong. I am just expressing myself, and I welcome other people's expressions of their truth." When it comes right down to it, everyone has their hand on one part of the endless animal of existence. If you think that someone has got their hands around a special truth, one that is truer than others, then at least know that you are the one making that distinction. If you suddenly see the oxygen mask dropping down due to a sudden loss of cabin pressure of confidence, it is your doing.

So were someone to say to me ,"Robert, you are quite arrogant," I can say, with a sparkle in my eyes and an open heart, "Why thank you for noticing! Thank you for your opinion." I may or may not take on board another person's opinion. It is my choice. Opinions, for me, exist on a horizontal axis: they are all equal in the sense that all colors of the rainbow exist as refractions of one light, and are thus all equal. Someone's opinion of me does not cause me to collapse, to become small and timid, or to betray my truth. I just say, "Thank you for your opinion."

I discovered that when I no longer tried to be right and I wasn't afraid of being wrong, when I built my horizontal axis of opinion — then I never had to be defensive. What would I defend? My opinion? Not hardly. It's just another opinion, and I change mine all the time. Without this defense against others, I became much more playful. Being playful, I can remain open. Remaining open, I can stay connected to myself and others. It is this connection with self and others that creates the channels for authentic relationship and communication.

Suddenly, Dana exploded. She had been sitting quietly, meditatively, on a cushion on the floor, just to my right. She had been listening intently. Something was whirring in her deep brain. Then, the monsoon:

"Oh my God! I just got it! No one is the boss of my thoughts!!"

Just as in the instant after the crack of thunder, there was throughout the room a deafening silence. Then, a roar. A roar of laughter and joy and celebration! I couldn't stop laughing! (My younger sister, Sandra, used to say "You are not the boss of me!" every time I'd try to get her to clean up my room or do something for me.)

Dana was glowing. She was a house on fire. She was drop-dead gorgeous in that moment of her epiphany. At the risk of putting words in her mouth, or of telling her what her opinion is, I will say Dana got that everything she had come to believe about herself, courtesy of other people, was not real, was not "gospel." It was just their opinion, and their opinion was not the boss of her thoughts.

She was now free to have her own opinion of herself, thank you very much. It is a fitting end to tell you that Dana's last talk of the workshop was titled, "I am the smartest person in the world."

The Choice To Be Authentic

Linley Anderson

It was the last session of Robert's workshop and we were to give our final talk. As each successive participant spoke, I shrank smaller and smaller. I had nothing to say. Everything was already being said, and better than I ever could. I loved every person over and over again as they stood so bravely and spoke so truthfully.

After each speaker finished, I held back and waited, not wanting to be next, not knowing what to say. Robert had said to wait — wait as long as it took. There would always be something to say. It would always come. So I waited. Then, up through the waves of panic bobbed a succession of reckless images bursting free from the places I'd so carefully hidden them.

The bewildered four-year old sobbing in the corner — a bright red ruler imprint smarting across the back of her legs. *Don't talk*, she decides, *it's safer.*

The car brakes screech, a loud bang, then a calf catapults down the road, her broken legs flailing. The little girl's screams are cut short as her mother turns and slaps her face. *Don't express fear,* she tells herself, *it's safer.*

She stands outside the classroom, face burning with shame, as the year seven teacher punctuates his lecture with penetrating silences. It's unwise, he threatens, to call your headmaster father "dad" when he visits the class. *Don't be yourself*, she whispers inwardly, *it's not safe.*

The final speaker on the high school debating team stands, frozen in mid-sentence. Just one minute ago it was all sewn up, she was on the home straight, they had won. Now there was just a furious hot rush in her ears. Someone mouths prompts but it's a foreign language. Nothing made sense. *You're not good enough to speak*, she admonished herself.

The adolescent girl in the swimming pool change-rooms. Her tightly held towel shields her shame as she turns away from curious eyes. Her asymmetrical breasts — one tiny and childishly bud-like, the other womanly full and rounded — were certain proof that she didn't deserve to exist. *God doesn't love you*, she tells herself.

These images had surfaced as a result of an earlier exercise with Robert. We had reflected on life events and the resulting self-limiting decisions we made about our worthiness to stand and speak our truth. As these events and the decisions I made washed over me, a new feeling started to arise. I've had this feeling before but I didn't know its name. It's like a swirl of energy that surges up from my feet and wraps itself warmly around my heart. Tears prickle just behind my eyes and my heart sings *Yes!* It was there when I swam my best (but didn't win) in the state finals, and my dad hugged me for trying. It was there when I held my newborn twins after a long and difficult pregnancy. It was there as I fled from an abusive husband. It was there as I made peace with my dying mother-in-law who had refused to see me for 25 years. And it was here, now. Robert calls it authenticity, "full access to one's inexhaustible inner resource of creative and expressive power."

As I stood to take my turn and offer my final talk of the weekend, a realization was dawning. I saw that in those moments when I turned away from who I really was, I had consciously made a choice. I had listened to others, believed negative thoughts, and ignored my own *Yes!* So, I could choose again and decide who I really was. And every moment is a new opportunity to make this choice over and over again — the choice to be authentic.

So, I stood and walked the few steps to the center of the room. Then I breathed deeply, grounded myself, took time to gather in my focus, let my gaze softly connect with those seated around me and, from the depths of my heart, told them just that.

I have no idea what's next for me but I carry Robert's precious gift. My relationship with myself and others is now truly and clearly guided from that re-discovered place within. I have had powerful, first hand experience of an incredibly nurturing and affirming learning process, and I know this is how I want to teach and reach others.

Commentary

"When we were children, we used to think that when we were grown-up we would no longer be vulnerable. But to grow up is to accept vulnerability ... to be alive is to be vulnerable."
Madeleine L'Engle

Throughout the workshop, Lin was quiet. She was attentive. She worked thoughtfully in the notebook. She spoke when it was her turn. She was quiet throughout.

There are different kinds of quiet. There is a quiet that portends something huge. Years ago, I lived in an Indian ashram. I remember the stillness, the quiet of that place just before an all-hell-breaking-loose monsoon would fall like an ocean for days on end without relief. Lin was that kind of quiet. Within her, I believe, something huge, enormous, and wild was brewing.

And then it came forth, quietly, but with stunning power and beauty.

In her essay, Lin describes how she gathered herself and her desire to be free of the past with the courage of the present, how she walked the few steps from her chair to the center of the room, how she breathed deeply, how she readied herself to bring forth in words her truth. She says with the simplicity that only truth can carry "from the depths of my heart, I told them just that."

And that was that. She told us just that. And then, quietly, she sat down. It was very quiet for a long time in that room. I was there, and it seemed that we had to be quiet to honor and appreciate what had just happened. Lin is one gutsy and beautiful lady.

Vulnerability has a bad rap, in that we often think it means to be weak and defenseless. If we are vulnerable, we will be hurt, enslaved, taken advantage of. But, as Lin showed, the safest place, the strongest place, the truest place ... is vulnerability.

Here, I want to introduce a single vital principle, one that makes Speak Truthfully a powerful catalyst for accomplishment, healing, and freedom: authentic connection.

Authentic connection means that you touch your audience by speaking from your heart to theirs, in a simple, direct manner. You look in their eyes and you tell the truth. Authentic connection has a precise formula:

Authentic Connection = Intimacy With Self + Vulnerability With Others

Intimacy with self implies a willingness and capacity to know oneself from the inside out, deeply; one must excavate through layers of repression, other people's ideas and beliefs, fears and inhibitions to a dynamic place of genuine enthusiasm for one's life, for one's speaking. Yes, there is a depth within each of us that connects us, as individuals, to the whole; not just to others, but to all of nature, to the Earth, to the Cosmos. We open ourselves to this depth, and then we receive what is already there, within us, waiting to be expressed. This is how we become most fully our unique self, while being most fully connected to others and to life.

Vulnerability with others implies a willingness and capacity to see and be seen; to stand in front of others fully seeing them, and allowing them to see you, without putting up masks or barriers behind which to hide or distort our genuine presence. Vulnerability is risky business, at best; we scarcely open ourselves all the way with our spouse or partner, how in the world can we do this in front of people we don't even know, and maybe hundreds of them? We can, and we want to. It is this quality of establishing a connection with oneself and one's audience that creates the channels through which communication — distinct from information — is transmitted. It is a matter of embodying one's message, rather than presenting information.

The challenge of authentic connection reveals and heals any impediments to a passionate, inspiring speaking of one's truthful, purposeful message. This is what sets people free, and this is what makes them great public speakers whose every word, gesture and silence is overflowing with the inspirational flavors of authenticity and integrity.

When I emailed Lin my edited version of her essay, I added a comment.

Flawlessly beautiful and authentic. I believe your essay by itself will offer healing and new life to thousands!

She wrote back.

I've got to tell you — this (writing) was a very clarifying and cathartic experience for me. The hardest part was allowing what I really had to say to come without that nasty critic jumping in all the time and telling me I'm actually total crap.

Actually, her inner critic is total crap. Lin is wonderful.

Roar

Kate Bezar

I grew up in New Zealand, a very good girl. I always studied hard, got great marks and did what was expected of me. I loved painting and English, but went on to study the far more sensible option of chemistry at university. In my final year I was offered the choice of a career with the Ministry of Foreign Affairs and Trade (on a path to becoming an ambassador) or a management consultant for a U.S. company based in Australia. I chose the latter. Apparently I had landed the “dream” job. For four years I worked on projects to improve the bottom lines of airlines, mining giants and banks, but the bottom line for me was that it didn’t *mean* anything. The problem was it seemed to mean a lot to everyone else.

I’m truly embarrassed to admit that what had mattered most to me my whole life, was what other people thought. I had never really considered what I really wanted, but ever-so-softly a voice inside my heart kept saying *But it doesn’t mean anything. Are you proud of what you’re doing? Is this it? I don’t think so, I think you’ve got a whole heap more to offer the world than this.* Eventually I listened to it.

It took me a while to extricate myself from the fantastic salary, extensive travel and the incomprehension of friends and family. I burnt my suits and heels, and took off traveling leaving the “me” I thought I was behind. I was on a mission to find what was truly “me” in the world. I did short courses in architecture and curating. I drew and painted for days on end. I wrote copious amounts in journals and I even thought I might become a yacht-designer for a while. But nothing sang true for me. Nothing made me so excited I couldn’t sleep at night. Nothing felt like the most natural thing in the world for me to be doing.

That was until I walked into a newsagent one damp evening wanting to buy a magazine and walked out empty-handed. I may have been empty-handed but I was exploding with excitement because I finally knew what I was going to do. I was going to create a magazine for people like me. *Dumbo feather* is the result.

I take star signs with little more than a grain of salt — unless of course they forecast extraordinary good fortune, knights in shining armor, and eternal happiness — in which case I’m sure they’re spot on. I had never thought myself a typical Leo either. Leos are the attention-loving, confidence-oozing sign of the zodiac, all mane, swagger, and roar.

Not so this little girl. All my life I've been the quiet one, the shy one, always far happier engrossed in the pages of a book than telling stories myself. Whenever I tried to tell stories I'd lose my way under the weight of the expectations of others, delivering a punch line with about as much oomph as a virgin daiquiri. I've always been hugely envious of those who could hold a room, or even just a cluster of people, in their thrall. I tended to choose people like that as friends so that they'd assume that role and I wouldn't have to. I was far, far happier sitting back listening to others.

Perhaps that was one of the reasons why, when I came up with the idea for *Dumbo feather*, it resonated so strongly. This was my chance to take up my favored position as listener. All I had to do was choose the most fascinating people, ask them some probing questions and then sit back and listen. OK, there's a little bit more to it than that, but that was a huge part of its appeal. I could just hang out behind the scenes and be entertained. That theory worked for the first couple of years. As *Dumbo feather's* editor, I wrote a note to readers every issue but nowhere in its pages was the story of how *Dumbo feather* came to be, and nowhere was I identified as its founder, although a savvy reader could have put two and two together and figured it out if they were so inclined.

Then gradually I began to get asked to speak at various forums on themes as varied as "finding your passion" and "the perils and pleasures of self-publishing." My initial resistance was huge, but then I thought, I ask the people I profile in *Dumbo feather* to do this, to tell their stories, so who am I to shy away from it myself? The talks were never to more than two hundred or so people and the feedback I received was always positive; nothing stellar, just fine. One day I checked my phone messages and there was one from a guy called Andrew who'd hosted me as a speaker before asking if I'd mind doing a similar thing again, only this time the audience would be over 3,000 people and I'd have 45 minutes with them.

Three thousand people, 45 minutes, at the Sydney Convention Center. A very, very, very big part of me wanted to say *Thanks ever so much for asking, but I really think you've got the wrong girl.* Then another part kicked in. It realized what an extraordinary privilege it would be to have that amount of time with that many individuals. I got to thinking about what I could use such an immense opportunity for. I came back to my dream to encourage individuals to be just that, individuals, living the most authentic, passionate lives possible. I truly believe, because I know from personal experience that it's true, that you will never be happy nor successful if you are not true to yourself. As Bill Cosby once said, "I don't know what the key to success is, but the key to failure is trying to please everybody."

Most of the other speakers at the Convention Center were designers showcasing their work. I was going to give the audience a bit of a geometry lesson instead, using the analogy that we're all essentially a star but sometimes that star can get its edges pulled out of shape as we try to be what we believe others want or expect us to be, with the end result usually just a messy splodge. I walked up onto that stage with adrenaline coursing through my veins and heart going a million miles an hour. I spoke from my heart for 45 minutes and *loved* it. So did they. Within minutes of leaving I was receiving texts from friends of friends who'd been there and people were posting notes on my website. I still receive the occasional email from someone who was in that audience saying that my words inspired them to seek the true them. That was my first taste of the power of authentic speaking and I'd caught sight of the Leo in me for sure. I heard myself roar.

But then, in subsequent talks I failed to capture that same feeling and essence. I fell back into my same old fears and patterns of trying to please others and be what I thought they wanted me to be. I'd water down my words so that they'd be less likely to polarize, but in the process lose all impact. So, when Robert invited me to participate in his Speak Truthfully course I jumped at the chance to find my way back to that place of authenticity and the ability to speak from my heart without censure. The timing couldn't have been better, as I was scheduled to give another talk to a group of engineers and later to be interviewed on ABC Radio as well as host a couple of Evenings for *Dumbo feather* & Friends; salons for the *Dumbo feather* community of people to meet and get to know each other.

Robert is an incredible speaker and human being and a lot of his impact is because he leads by example. You watch Robert and go, *I want what he's got.* Well I did anyway. But he was also extremely good at helping each individual in our group find their own unique voice; heaven forbid we'd all walk out talking like Robert Rabbin! Robert helped me internalize what I knew intellectually to be true and even what I'd preached to others: you can never be what others want you to be, you can only be you. So why not be the truest you possible? He helped me see and go beyond my fears to a place where I think I even cracked a funny and people laughed. I told a story and people listened. I made a complete ass of myself and loved it. I did it without adrenaline powering me along, but just with a few fluttery butterflies for company instead.

Best of all he made me roar, literally and metaphorically. In fact, he asked me to teach the others in the group how to roar, too. I stood in front of the class and, one by one, each participant came to stand with me. We'd face each other and then roar our heads off and our lungs out! It felt awesome.

It's so vital that we all become better at roaring; that I roar my story, that the people I invite to share their stories through *Dumbo feather* roar theirs, and that you roar yours as well, because in doing so, we inspire others to roar too.

Commentary

"But Oz never did give nothing to the Tin Man
That he didn't, didn't already have ..."
"Tin Man," America

As Kate was leading her roaring session in the workshop, I thought, *Now, there's some shakti!* Shakti is a Sanskrit word which refers to the creative power and expressive potential inherent in the universe, and from which all things derive their life and consciousness. Or, as one workshop participant in Perth said, "My experience of shakti is amazing power and quiet passion." Our message, meaning, and purpose are conveyed as much by our shakti — our spirit, our life-force — as by our words. Speaking with shakti is not dissimilar from how a martial artist gathers and focuses *chi*, energy, before striking through a concrete block. The force of the blow isn't about muscle strength, it's about spiritual strength, gathered and focused intensity. Our speaking power and force is not about volume, it's about the way we project our words and meaning with our shakti, about force and thrust from the center of our being.

Shakti is also what powers our capacity to change and transform and grow; it's what we need in order to choose confidence, to create new ways of being and speaking. A Ferrari needs gas to go, and we need shakti to speak. When I introduce this term in my workshops, I say that almost all of the "issues" people have around public speaking are due to a poverty of shakti, a suppression of this innate creative and expressive power.

It's easy for people to grasp this idea of shakti and then translate it to their own experience. Everyone I've ever worked with has a point of reference for understanding and experiencing shakti. Some experience it while in nature, others listening to music or singing. Childbirth, hang-gliding, gardening, sports, playing with children — the energy of life flows and flows through all of creation and is always available to us as tremendous strength and power, a kind of invincibility and certainty, not of our point of view or beliefs, but of our very being, of our capacity for creative self-expression.

The meditation teacher with whom I studied for 10 years loved to tell stories. The following story was one of his favorites, from the Sufi tradition. I didn't know then, so many years ago, that the morale of this story would be as pertinent to authenticity and power in the realm of public speaking as it was to authenticity and power in the realm of human being. Oh, wait. They are one and the same!

Once there was a great lioness that went hunting with her newborn cub. While chasing and attacking a flock of sheep, the she-lion made a wrong move, fell off a cliff, and died. The cub was left without a mother and so joins the flock of sheep, and they take him in as one of them. As the years passed, the cub becomes an adult, but it now behaves like a sheep. It eats grass, makes a bleating sound, and has a fear of all other animals. He walks around like a sheep and ba-a-a-a's like a sheep. He joins in as they talk about the stock market, complain about the hard work at the office, and how life is boring — you know, the stuff that sheep do all the time. Life goes on.

One day an old lion standing on a hilltop sees this horrendous sight and is outraged. It's as if this young lion is bringing shame to the whole race of lions. "What the hell is this guy doing down there? He should be eating them, not eating *with* them!" He runs down into the valley, kills a couple of sheep, and grabs the young lion, who is sure he will also be killed. But of course the old lion doesn't kill him. Instead he takes him to a pool of water and forces him to look at his reflection. The sheepish lion thinks he's going to see a sheep, but he doesn't. He sees a lion. And then the older lion grabs a piece of meat from a dead sheep and feeds it to him. This is like cannibalism to the young lion, so he's horrified. But he eats it, and after a couple of bites he decides the meat doesn't taste so bad.

And then the old lion says, And now you are going to roar. He shows him: ROAAAR!!! Now you do it.

The young lion lets out a feeble Roaa-ba-a-a.

NO, NO!

So they work at it for a long time, and after many attempts, the young lion manages to give a great ROOOAAAAAAAAAR! That is the roar of awakening. The Sufis say it is the roar of a human being who discovers his true nature.

Adding another chapter to this traditional Sufi story, I want to say that one's true nature, in Speak Truthfully terms, is one's truth. I define one's truth as "a transparent telling of this is what I think and feel; this is what I want and what I don't want." Telling the truth is what keeps our soul whole and our integrity intact. Let's not confuse one's truth with Truth. I'm suspicious of the latter. I don't know about Truth, and the people who do, the people who claim to know The Truth, well, they make me nervous. But "one's truth" is the window to our character, to our uniqueness, to our passions in life. Our honest and undefended thoughts and feelings, wants and not-wants, are always and ever-changing, growing, evolving — this dynamic truth is what makes us "us," what gives us our distinctive look and feel and smell. We cannot be afraid of our truth, we cannot be afraid of our own self. It is, after all, just another opinion — not better or worse, not bigger or smaller — just another opinion. But it is ours. It is us.

The Sufi poet Jelaluddin Rumi once sang, as he sang all his poems, never writing them, "There is one thing that we all must do. If we do everything else but that one thing, we will be lost. And if we do nothing else but that one thing, we will have lived a glorious life." What is this one thing we must do, that no one else but us can do? To find this, to speak this: Is this not our *roar*? Is this not, as Kate says, "being true to yourself"? How can our speaking be true, if we are not first true to ourself? How can truth come from a lie? How can a lion be born to a sheep?

I did ask Kate to tutor the others in *roaring*. Every workshop is distinctive, and in every workshop I end up inventing one or more activities or exercises, inspired and guided by the group. This is the only time we roared like this! Kate called each of the other participants, one at a time in turn, to come stand with her in the front of the room. They would then face each other. I watched Kate's eyes grab the eyes of her roaring partner. I watched her summon the energy and courage of the Lion, and then, together, she and her fellow lion would start roaring, and roared and roared until they laughed and cried and yelled and roared some more.

When she was done, when they were done, I don't think there was a single sheep within a million miles.

Open Plan Living

Michael Jensen

I never expected when I attended Speak Truthfully that I would end up thinking about drawing. You see, I loved to draw as a child but I had not expected to remember how much I enjoyed it (and secretly still missed it). Knowing Robert and the kind of person and facilitator that he is, I had expected to have fun. I expected that I would come away with some good speaking tips and reminders of what makes a good presentation. But to be honest, I had a little bit of arrogance in me that said, *I'm already a pretty good presenter*. In fact I like speaking in front of people. I even like being looked at and being the center of attention (the product of being an only child?). I'd even liked this at school. I was the kid who, when given a choice between giving a presentation or submitting a piece of written work, would always go for the option of standing up in front the class so I could have everyone's attention.

The night before the workshop, I thought, *This will be good. Good, but not earth-shattering*. Little did I know that for me the experience of being part of Robert's course was definitely not just about speaking. Ever done a course where you think it's about one thing and then you find out it's really about something else completely? Like the time I did a course in pottery. What I thought was a course about a potter's wheel and wet lumps of clay turned out to be about slowing down, slowing right down, and learning to not be a perfectionist. Same thing with this.

Speak Truthfully came along when I was at a bit of a crossroads in my life and career but was still only dimly aware of it. I was just beginning to face some big questions: Was I going to continue in my career and the business I was building? And what about finding meaning and authenticity in what I was doing? I took these questions to the class, and it was these questions that triggered the memory of my boyhood drawings and the joy I associated with them, reminding me of the importance of certain things.

But the story really began about six months before, in early 2007.

My wife and I had decided to sell our house and move on. Our kids had grown up and moved out to find their own places in the world. It left us feeling lost about *our* place in the world. Except now when I think about it, we had both been feeling pretty displaced for quite a while, but the absence of our boys sharpened the loss of connection to them, and the big house reminded us of the emptiness that was created and of our own changing lives. One morning my wife, being far more intuitive and decisive (some would say impulsive) than I, rolled over in bed to look at me and announced, "It's time to move on." Not getting the full drift and implications of her statement, I assumed she meant something such as getting out of bed and taking the dogs for their morning walk. Uh, no.

Soon our house was on the market. But change does not come easily, especially for someone who has lived in the same house for 23 years. Still, the decision was made and a momentum for movement was created. However, we found that there was almost instantly a series of obstacles, making the next steps difficult. Letting go of this house, one of the mainstays of security in our life, something that we had invested our emotions, our memories, and our money in, was very difficult. At times it even felt like the house did not want to let go of us! Right up to the auction, it creaked and groaned in the night, and banged its doors to keep us awake, right up to the eventful day. As it turned out, the sale of our house was only the beginning of massive change in each of our lives. The auction and sale of our house echoed through other parts of our lives. For me it was the catalyst of further change in my career and my business.

Soon things started to go wrong. My business partner and I discovered that our recently departed bookkeeper had not performed diligently when completing the tax forms, paying the creditors, and reconciling the bank statements. In my business as a mediator and conflict consultant, I found that new projects and activities that we had taken on, more for reasons of making extra money and not reflecting the core of our work, were going seriously wrong. Other clients, who for a long time had been happy with my work, were now becoming angry with me. I was becoming concerned about the viability of my business. And then, just before my wife and I went on holidays, my accountant dropped a further bombshell: a hefty tax bill of $35,000 that we had not anticipated, which was the result of having our heads in the sand and not bothering to open our eyes to a part of a business we had never really enjoyed doing: the finances and accounting.

Sometimes you go through times where you feel like you're being led, where life's trying to tell you that it's time to lift your head out of the sand. It does this in all kinds of weird ways: accidents, illnesses, repeated bad news, failures, losing things like your wallet, having your car towed away in a clearway zone right before an important job interview. When these things happen, it doesn't feel like you're being led, it feels more like you're being persecuted! That's when life, God, or whatever you want to call it comes knocking loudly on your front door to come out and face the white stare of the world, yet all you want to do is put more locks on the doors and keep on doing what you've always done. The last thing I wanted to do was come out and walk boldly down some new street of authentic living!

Robert refers often to this idea of "living out loud" as a way of speaking up with our authentic voice, reflecting our authentic life. In the course notebook, he's put a poem by Lucille Clifton, as an example of authenticity. The final two lines are, "I throw my fierce thigh high over the rump of the day, and honey, I ride, I ride … ." As a mediator I've always tried to help other people speak up and find their authentic voice. Where was mine?

In his little house in Richmond on a Sunday morning a small group of us gathered together for the first day of the workshop. We were nervous, not just because we hadn't met each other and knew that soon we would be sharing our thoughts and feelings with one another, but also because of the video camera positioned conspicuously at the end of the room. I knew intuitively that this was not just about public speaking. This was about being with ourselves. When you get past the introductions and the "elevator" speeches about what we do and what we have achieved in our lives and how many kids we've got — there is just *you.*

Throughout the day Robert was cracking jokes about the unfathomable eccentricity of Australian culture and language. Through his humour and his example of confidently sharing his own amazing life he encouraged us to connect with the other "strangers" in the group, in the same way we would need to speak to our audiences in our presentations or conversations. Immediately I felt that all the well-worn and well-rehearsed openings and remarks were not appropriate here, so I initially felt uncomfortable with this vulnerability. But with the support of the people, the atmosphere, Robert's self-deprecating humor and his gentle listening, I was inspired to listen to myself, and to look for a voice that belonged to my authentic self. For someone who is often busy playing different roles and hiding behind lots of masks, that kind of awakening can be … searing!

But we learned to connect with one another. We began with silence and then, looking into the eyes and faces of the people, we started to speak, from the heart, from a place of real sharing and vulnerability.

One of the presentations we did that day was about being playful and silly, a side of me that I learned to suppress through years of maintaining the public persona of a calm, keeps-it-together-under-pressure lawyer. In fact I'm not a cool, cerebral person at all, as my wife will tell you after two glasses of wine. I am and always have been a spontaneous, emotional child! I experienced a wonderful sense of freedom in being able to do this in front of people I knew for all of four hours. And then, seeing myself on camera, I thought, *That playful clown isn't so bad after all! What would happen if he came out more?*

On that day one of the things I learned is that when you experience the freedom of speaking authentically, without fear of censure or judgment, you find the inspiration to do more, to keep going, like the lady in the poem who throws her leg over the rump of life and shouts, *Honey, I ride, I ride*. The more you speak authentically, the more you ride, the more you communicate openly and without fear, the more you realize that this is natural, it's how we really ought to be! It's like having a love of Michael Jackson's music video clips like "The Thriller." You love practicing the moves at home on a Saturday afternoon when everyone's out shopping. There's just you, the dog, and the stereo. But you secretly want to dance your "thriller" moves at work with your colleagues and get them to join in (weird, I know, but that is a secret fantasy I have). I suppose my point is that when you experience being authentic you want more of it — and you wish others would join in as well. God how I wish that people

I deal with in business — my colleagues, my clients, and the parties in the mediation disputes — could understand that the choice is simple, though I'm not saying easy! The simple choice is this: be real.

As I reflected on the experience of authenticity in my own life, I realized that I do not want to have separate rooms in my life, each one for a different part of my life. I want the integration and wholeness of authenticity: open plan living instead of lots of little box-like rooms, one for each of our various roles. I think everyone yearns for open plan living.

I'll always remember the morning of the workshop where Robert invited us to consider the last time that each of us had expressed ourselves creatively and authentically. In responding to that invitation, I connected with a deeper part of myself, and the recollection of that experience was like the front door of my house being flung open and the memory of my childhood pastime came flooding back, like the late afternoon sun flooding into the house through open doors. There I was as a child drawing with a pencil and paper, and the lines on that paper were flowing as if from a river of forceful creativity and there was no hint of self-criticism or judgment. And I remembered how when I was engrossed in that drawing I was also truly engrossed in the moment — I knew no sense of time or self.

I don't know where that image came from or why it came back so strongly, but it left me so moved and full of grief that I felt instantly sad and determined to connect with that experience again, determined to be truly myself, truly powerful and truly creative.

Working with Robert made me realize that to be totally engaged with people and with what you are doing in the moment is the key to finding your uniqueness and power as an individual. Most of the time I struggle to be fully present and aware in the moment. Like most people there are huge parcels of time when I savor the relief at the end of the activity I am performing rather than the experience of the activity itself. Speak Truthfully is the bridge from our commonplace experiences of non-engagement to that place where we find our power as individuals.

Commentary

"I used to draw when I was a kid.
At 15 years of age, I was told that I couldn't make a living by drawing,
that I should go to law school. I never drew again.
When I think of authenticity, I am sad, because
I've never been as authentic as when I was drawing."
Mike Jensen

I remember reading an anecdote about a woman who was going off to work one evening. As she kissed her young daughter good-bye, the little girl asked, "Mommy, what is it you do again?"

Her mother, who taught art at a local college, said, "Honey, I teach grown-ups how to paint."

The little girl thought for a moment and then asked, incredulously, "You mean, they forget how?"

Yes, sweetheart, I'm sorry to say, we forget how.

When we stop painting, we forget how. When we stop drawing, we forget how. When we stop dancing and singing, we forget how. When we stop dreaming, we forget how. When we stop learning, we forget how. When we stop growing, we forget how. When we stop risking, we forget how. When we stop exploring and inventing, we forget how.

When we stop being and believing in ourselves, we forget how. When we stop believing in each other, we forget how.

When we stop being generous, and kind, and big-hearted, we forget how. When we stop expressing our own beauty and strength and creativity, we forget how. When we stop playing with children and animals, we forget how.

When we stop being bold and daring and big and brash and wild, we forget how. When we stop being vulnerable and open and tender and caring, we forget how. When we stop savoring every single second of life, we forget how.

When we stop choosing confidence and courage, we forget how.

When we stop listening, we forget how. When we stop loving and making love, we forget how.

When we stop telling our truth, we forget how. Most tragically, when we stop speaking authentically, we forget how.

Therefore, don't ever stop doing these things. Ever. For any reason. Keep doing them, no matter what. Another person's life grammar? Fuhgedaboutit. Make your own stylebook.

Playing With Passion

Suzanne Saad

My eldest sister Lisa died when I was twelve years of age. Fifteen years later it still remains the single most defining experience of my life. By that I mean not just the impact of her death, but the indelible impression her life continues to have on me. The privilege of knowing Lisa was instrumental in shaping who I am, my worldview and the contribution I aspire to make in the world. Many of the details of memories I have of her have faded over time, but what remains, as clear as ever, as if etched in my heart, is her particular quality of energy, what her personal presence felt like. Her unique light. That's what lives on. It was a deep realization for me to see what a human life eventually boils down to, that what will stay with people is *the feeling of being with you.*

When I read the tagline of the Speak Truthfully course, "YOU are the message!," it resonated deeply with me. I signed up for the workshop knowing the truth of the statement. In fact, the core message I convey through my work with people is t*o see, value, and express their own individuality as their own unique contribution to the world*. My intention in the workshop was really about deepening my own integrity, taking the next step to more fully walk my own talk. My experience with Lisa really showed me that the most meaningful thing we can give another is our own unique presence. If I am going to ask that of my clients, than I want to be the best example possible of doing exactly that myself!

Enter Mr. Robert Rabbin. "Here I am," he says, not so much in those words, but through his demeanor, his confident inner and outer posture, the quality of his speech and the look in his eyes. Yes! My heart sang at the spark of recognition: I want more of that! But how do I get it? That was my question. I truly believe the qualities we admire in others already exist as potential within ourselves. So how could I, as Robert seemed to be doing, access that part of me that is so present with people, connecting strongly, heart open and fully visible, standing in the truth of who I am, without reservation or qualification, playfully riding every minute of it?

Robert highlighted the fact that we all know how to be purely authentic as we all do it somewhere, with someone, in someway in our lives. So his question was, why should it be any different when it comes to public speaking? Good point. So I thought, what makes me squelch my full self a little or a lot, depending on the company I'm in?

It came down to fearing that my audience would judge me as being weird. Weird for the way I look and weird for the passions and views I hold and wish to share. That was the root of what was holding me back from completely stepping into my individuality, from showing up with absolute self-assurance and presence.

Let me explain. While my right eye is straight, I have a turn in my left eye — they call it "wall-eyed" because it looks like my left eye is looking at the wall rather than looking straight at you. While it has the capacity to come in straight, it spends most of its time resting slightly to the left. This has been the source of awkward self-consciousness for me over the years. It was really my own personal pink elephant that I would bring into every room I ever went into.

In truth, over the years, only a hand full of people have questioned me directly about my eye: "Are you looking at me or over there?" Most people never say a thing about it. But even so, I would cringe internally when I would sometimes notice, in my acute self-consciousness, that people had a confused look on their face, taking a double look trying to work out what's up with my eyes. Since neither of us would actually say anything out loud about it, my inner critic had free reign. "See, you do look weird, just as you anticipated. Here we go again, another person has noticed how strange you look. 'You sures is ugly.'" (Yes, my inner critic would frequently speak in an African-American accent, often repeating this quote from the movie *The Color Purple*.)

In terms of my passions and views … I started out on a conventional path with a Bachelor of Arts and Bachelor of Commerce from the University of Sydney with a major in Human Resource Management. I knew I wanted to work within the areas of motivation and development of people and so was happy with this direction. Yet, I felt I wanted something more. This desire led me to gain qualifications in both the Aura-Soma® Color System and Transpersonal Art Therapy.

I am passionate about both these modalities as tools for self-awareness and growth. In both my personal work and work with clients, I have seen over and over the power of color and artistic expression as a means to connect to our unique inner world, to create a meaningful vision, to clarify and embody our personal strengths and values, and as resources for dealing with life challenges. These modalities also help us to celebrate our individual past, present and future story and see our place in relationship to everyone else.

However, using the right-brain tools of color and art for such purposes is little understood in mainstream circles. So, as I bring these valuable tools to the corporate arena through my business *breathe HR*, I am confronted with who misunderstand and even dismiss the efficacy of my work, branding the tools as "weird or too new-age." Being human, sometimes hearing such opinions, which comes with the territory of offering innovative, creative, and cutting-edge approaches, can become tiring. If only they could see! As Einstein said "It is harder to crack a prejudice than an atom."

Thankfully, Robert, offered the key for me to free me from my own limited perceptions. When you are ready to hear something, the words resonate so strongly, like a sounding bell, marking a change of being. That's what happened when I heard Robert say: "If we are not trying to be right and not afraid to be wrong, all that is left is play. I am just playing with my opinions. I am not defending them, nor attacking someone else's. I am just expressing my truth. I have a whole lot of confidence in who I am, which allows me to play in life."

Quite frankly, I laughed at myself, realizing how obvious yet genius a point he was making — surely I should have already known that myself! In fact, it reminded me of one of my favorite quotes by Oscar Wilde, "Life is too important to be taken seriously." So, why did I seem to take myself so seriously when it came to people's opinions about my eye and my chosen vocation? The idea of playing was the truth that set me free. Free to stand more firmly in the truth of who I am — yes, this is my eye and, yes, these are my opinions, and I'm quite happy for you to have your opinions about them — come on let's play.

And so this experience brings me back to Lisa again. She was the first person to teach me how important play is. She was never too old to play with me. She'd once told me, "My inner five-year-old is just below the surface; make sure you never lose yours either." Wise woman! As an adult, when I reflected back on her life, the key message of her life to me was "live with heart" — she did absolutely everything with pure heart. My own bottom line in life was greatly shaped by my observations of her. For me, my litmus test of a day well-lived is whether I experience light-heartedness. And it is my opinion that true light-heartedness comes from *creating with passion your own work of heART to contribute to the world.* When I share this idea with others, I then show them how I play with the word passion:

I be myself so I can *pass-I-on.*
Then, ideally *on-I-pass* to others
before *I-pass-on.*

In this way, I can say Speak Truthfully ignited more passion in my life. As I more consciously come from the spirit of play, I am willing to more directly share who I am with others. The opinions of others are no longer an internal burden; rather, they excite my favorite feeling of light-heartedness

within me as they serve to remind me that we are all just playing!
So, what did Robert's unique presence in his course give me? The greater integrity I came for. I won't be here forever so *here I am* now with you!

Commentary

"You're only given a little spark of madness. You mustn't lose it."
Robin Williams

Suzanne is profoundly playful, a true player, and it is thrilling to watch her own the stage with her energy, zeal, and pure passionate intensity! She came to the workshop, as she says, wanting to more fully "access that part of me that is so present with people, connecting strongly, heart open and fully visible, standing in the truth of who I am, without reservation or qualification, playfully riding every minute of it."

Playfully. That single word might escape our notice, or it may not immediately appear to be as important as I think it is. I think it's huge.

People in my workshops, and elsewhere, often comment on what they perceive to be my willingness to say anything, to not be afraid of making a mistake or of misstating something. They seem to like how "free" I am in my speaking. I tell them my secret: I am not trying to be right and I am not afraid of being wrong.

Most of my workshop participants and coaching clients evaluate their public speaking prowess through the filters of "good" and "bad" or "right" and "wrong." These frameworks are too limiting for RealTime Speakers; we are looking for something more expansive. We want to see how authentic we are being and how well we connect with our audience. The dynamic expression of your character and truth, your creative passions and shakti of your expressive power are not a good-bad, right-wrong proposition. If we are going to evaluate, let us do so by noticing the quality of our presence, awareness, openness, authenticity, and connection; by our clarity, courage, and confidence. When I play their talks for people to see themselves, I ask, "What do you notice?" That's it. I do not allow good and bad, right and wrong comments. I want people to totally shift their perspective on seeing themselves, and thus their perceptions on their speaking.

The good-bad, right-wrong polarity is a heavy, a too heavy, burden to carry through life. It will crush us. It will ruin us. It will kill us. We will live entombed in the fear of accusation, of "bad" and "wrong." Or we will be desperate for approval, speaking only for the vanity of "good" and "right."

Suffocation and slow death by badness and wrongness. Suffocation and slow death by rightness and goodness. (Excuse my grammar.)

If we speak defensively from behind a fortified façade, all our speaking is noise.

In our speaking, if we are not trying to be right or good, and we are not afraid of being wrong or bad, if we speak undefended and unguarded, seeking only to express our truth with authenticity and integrity, with clarity and courage, connected to self and others — if we speak in this way, what do we, inevitably, become?

Think about this for a minute. When I ask this in workshops, I get the feeling people have never considered this perspective: *I am not trying to be right, and I am not afraid of being wrong.*

What happens? What do we become?

PLAYFUL.

We become playful.

It's an amazing thing, isn't it, to be able to play with others, to express our opinion without needing to be right, without being afraid of being wrong, no need to defend or attack — just playing together knowing our expression is just that, and theirs is just that. When we play, we are connected, we enjoy, we explore, we learn, we grow, we have fun, we try new things. Imagine if our public speaking were full of these "playful" qualities. That's what I do when I speak: I play. The impact I make in my speaking has to do with openness, authenticity, and connection — with how playful I am.

I'm playful. That's why I am not afraid of forgetting something, or of losing my place, or of being asked something I don't know, or of having someone who is smarter than me correct something I say. I'm not afraid of people leaving and I'm not afraid of wild applause. In my speaking, nothing bad can ever happen, and nothing can ever go wrong. Isn't that liberating? I think so. Of course, the flip side of that coin is that nothing in my speaking can ever be right or good. Isn't that liberating? I think so.

Apparently, so does dear Suzanne.

Being playful does not mean we are childish or foolish. It does not mean we aren't wise, profound, learned, moving, sincere, serious, ferocious, delicate, tender, wild, sensual, erotic, intellectual, emotional, poetic, radical, or anything else.

It just means we are not trying to be right and we are not afraid of being wrong.

There is a tiny sub-culture, whose denizens are my "playful" teachers. I watch them, I study them, I breathe them in. They say things that, well, sometimes I just can't believe they said what they said. But they are smiling and playing, and serious and purposeful. They are not trying to be right, and they are not afraid of being wrong. They are exploring their creative imagination and expressive potential. They are speaking their way to artistic freedom. I love them. They terrify me. They challenge me. They piss me off. They thrill me. Hooray for them! Who are they?

Sketch and stand up comics, especially the improv kind. Jonathan Winters. Robin Williams. Richard Pryor. Rita Rudner. Wendy Liebman. Catherine Tate. Chris Rock. Billy Connolly.

Many people are defensive about some aspect of their appearance. One lady had really large hands, and she was always hiding them behind her back. I suggested that she see them as beautiful exotic Japanese fans, and use them as props. Play with them. Flaunt them. They are beautiful and fantastic. Make people jealous that they don't have these fan-hands. She was delighted with my idea, and suddenly a life-long habit of hiding her hands was transformed when she stopped guarding herself. Suzanne has a wall-eye. That's a hard thing to hide. She could have let that drive her underground into terminal hiding. She didn't. In the workshop, Suzanne asked for my opinion about how she ought to deal with this wall-eye in her talks. I said that people probably just wanted to know where to look, so I suggested she just say something simple to put people at their ease and tell them where to look. Then, it wouldn't be an issue. Suzanne came up with this ingenious, and playful, opening to her next talk:

"I'll start by pointing out that I have a real passion for looking at things from a variety of perspectives and angles. The thing is, my left eye has taken this way of seeing the world slightly left-of-center to an extreme; it wanders off from time to time to look at things by itself. Even I don't know when or where it will go! So for your reference, if you're not sure where I'm looking, and where you should look, pay attention to my right eye — it's the straight one. My left eye might be off on one of its walkabouts."

And then she continued with her talk as her charisma and playfulness enfolded the audience in delight.

Information Obsession

Lynn Berry

I've delivered many presentations, workshops, conference papers, and lectures; and yet, I so doubt myself that sometimes I sabotage what I'm doing, ending up personally devastated while my audience is bewildered. My self-doubts always prevented me from making a real connection with my audience.

My story is that I had low self-esteem. I'm going to tell you how I think this happened and how it has affected my public speaking. If I hadn't done the Speak Truthfully course, I wouldn't be at this point of self-realization. Part of the problem has been "being me."

In the workshop, Robert asked us to reflect on what we thought our impediments to speaking authentically were. I saw myself being boxed in and pressured to perform according to conventions. I thought of all the boxes I had collected and how these had programmed me to be something other than myself. Despite my rebelliousness as a teenager, they (teachers, parents) successfully molded me into a more conventional person. During my early years, being "me" wasn't acceptable. I wanted to have fun, to laugh, to be heard, but I was under the rule of "don't speak unless you're spoken to." I had to stay unnoticed, a nobody.

There have been outbreaks — like when I was a squatter on the edge of Amsterdam with a bunch of crooks and agreed to marry someone so he could live in Australia, or when I ran away to the snowfields to live with a man 25 years older than me. Even he turned out to be just another person who I let mould me. I've been living these programs most of life.

This programming has had the effect of imprisoning "me" behind various conventional disguises, compelling me to behave according to what others wanted for me, like embracing conventional careers. And I've maintained these disguises, afraid of being rejected if I didn't comply, afraid to truly express myself. I wanted people, my family in particular, to be proud of me, to acknowledge my achievements, to see me. I hid the things I knew they wouldn't have liked. When was I ever going to come out?

This partly explains why I hide behind lots of information when I give presentations. My preparation consists of gathering as much factual information as possible on the topic I'm to speak about, pages and pages of notes that I convert to slides for the PowerPoint format. And when I'm actually giving my talk, I concentrate so much on this information that I forget I'm talking to *people*.

I remember presenting information about speech technology to a select group of people from an organization. This presentation was one prepared by head office, although there was some freedom to delete or rearrange. I spoke about how speech recognition works — pretty complicated stuff. On and on I went, even after noticing that many of the people in my audience had that glazed look in their eyes, having retreated into their own inner world of thoughts and daydreams to escape the tedium of my presentation. I realized this, but I kept right on going with all my information!

I felt that I needed the "information" to be credible, and I was afraid that without it I would be seen as a failure, judged as not being smart and clever. The information was like a university degree for me: it was supposed to in some way certify that I was an expert. This conventional credibility would entitle me to respect, higher paying jobs, loftier status. I suppose when I really look at it, the more information I had at my disposal, the more I could overwhelm my audience with knowledge, and the more credible I would feel. I believed that my information would prove how knowledgeable I was; then I would be right. Yes, that's it: the tidal wave of information-based knowledge would make me feel legitimate, valuable, and worthy of respect. Worthiness is tied up with self-esteem. Even after earning a Dip. Art, B.A., and Ph.D., I wasn't all that convinced about "me." I still believed that I had to have lots of information. I thought that the quantity of my information is what counted.

In the workshop, Robert said that our impact as a speaker came not from information, but from connection, from authenticity. He said that before anyone was really going to listen to our content, they had to believe us, the speaker, and that was a matter of being vulnerable, of making a real-time connection with the audience. Previously I'd been concerned about the information and getting that right. But connecting with the audience is not easy, especially given my history of hiding behind information.

With the suggestion to be vulnerable, transparent, and present, I realized how very susceptible I had been to criticism, or perceived criticism, from my audience. This has a big impact on my self-confidence. When I would feel that people were not interested, things would really start to unravel. I feel myself starting to lose the thread, to lose the flow of the discussion; my energy drops to the point where I can't talk and hardly know what to say; my mouth becomes dry and my speech is unclear, it sounds almost like I'm stuttering. My face is hot, my heart is pounding and I feel terribly embarrassed. I know everyone else feels this too, and the whole room shudders.

What I really wanted is for everyone to like me, to enjoy listening to me, to feel that their time was well spent. Of course, these are good things; it's just that I went about it in the wrong way. I put mountains of information, other people's ideas, in front of me, trying to make a good impression with the content of my speaking, not the "me" of my speaking. I was afraid of being criticized, judged, and seen as inadequate. I wouldn't risk showing myself, which is a pattern that started a long time ago.

I'd be afraid to speak up when I didn't agree with what others said, being afraid to reveal my true colors. I'd be afraid to say that I was sorry, or afraid to reveal the emotion that I truly felt. This is what happened in many of my relationships. Some of the upheavals in my life have been because I didn't want to hurt someone either by saying no, or by saying how I felt, thereby allowing life to roll on with me being the unhappy participant until things blew up. It's been a roller coaster and it's been totally exhausting.

As I write this I find it hard to believe that I was unable to speak my truth. However, I wanted to be liked; I didn't want to cause trouble; I didn't want to hurt anyone. And yet despite my efforts to make this happen, the opposite happened.

In previous courses on speaking, the emphasis has been on the voice or on content, gliding over the real issues, at least *my* real issues. What I discovered through Speak Truthfully is that I've allowed criticism to unsettle me due to fear, low self-esteem, and lack of confidence. My information obsession was a cover for these feelings. I've also come to know that fear of speaking my truth and the inability to do so has caused me much pain. I'm very grateful that I've been prodded to see these things.

This is my now my challenge: to believe enough in myself so as to not need everyone to like me and to not be afraid of criticism. I need to decide that I can, safely and credibly, show "me," to speak from my heart, to say what I really think and feel. I can allow this now. I'm ready for the next step.

Commentary

"Where is the Life we have lost in living?
Where is the wisdom we have lost in knowledge?
Where is the knowledge we have lost in information?"
T. S. Eliot

Lynn, Lynn, Lynn — you are *gorgeous*! Thank you! Your essay is the Emancipation Proclamation for information slaves everywhere. We should frame your essay and hang it in every corporate boardroom and every meeting and training room in every company throughout the world!

People don't want more information — they've got plenty. As Gertrude Stein wrote, "Everybody gets so much information all day long that they lose their commonsense."

People don't want information from you, not right away. They want something else: they want to know you, they want to believe in you, to have faith in you and in who you say you are. Before you attempt to influence anyone, you need to establish enough trust to successfully deliver your message. A person's trust in "who you are" becomes the connection that is the conduit for your message. Before anyone allows you to influence them, they want to know, Who are you? Can I trust you? Are you credible and believable? Do you walk your own talk?

If people — whether a prospective customer, a board of directors, your staff, spouse, or 10,000 adoring fans — doubt your sincerity and credibility, they won't listen to you. They won't hear you. As speakers, our first job is to demonstrate our credibility, our believability, our authenticity. We've got to show up first. Lynn confesses, "This partly explains why I hide behind lots of information when I give presentations. I feel that I need the 'information' to be credible … " No. No. No.

Credibility comes from authenticity. People want to know, and trust, *us*. That's why we get up to speak with people, to show who we are. If we are only going to be tour guides for a PowerPoint, stay home. When people come to see us, to hear us, then we should show them us, not a PowerPoint. Many businesspeople confuse information with communication. Sydney J. Harris, an American journalist and author, sets us straight, "The two words 'information' and 'communication' are often used interchangeably, but they signify quite different things. Information is giving out; communication is getting through."

OK, there are different kinds of credibility, and we want to be mindful of all of them. Credibility with an audience is generated in many different ways, from what we wear to the pitch of our voice. It comes from our experience and achievements. It comes from careful research and the scholarship of our facts and figures. But these are subordinate to our authentic presence. We've got to learn how to show who we are, from way down deep. We've got to learn to tell the truth, then we'll be able to know who else is doing it.

Government officials, corporate executives, celebrities, sports figures — a day does not pass that some scandal of corruption, fraud, or deception doesn't make the front page of any newspaper. Let's set things straight: we are not victims in this. The light is always on. What people do is always visible. Maybe they aren't telling the truth, but we aren't listening for the truth. Their lies reflect and mirror ours. If we really want to, we can see with our light into the darkness that others may use to cloak and camouflage their speaking. As *we* begin to speak authentically and transparently, we begin to listen in the same way. This is how we begin to see who else speaks authentically, and who does not. But we've got to go first.

Once we get used to telling the truth, living and speaking authentically, then we get used to discerning the truth. You could say we are gifted with a subscription to next week's or next year's newspaper today. We'll know what hides unspoken in the darkness. For us, there are no scandals. There is no corruption. We are not surprised. We are not disappointed. But we've got to go first.

Late last year, I was invited by the visiting president of a U.S. company to listen to his keynote address to an international conference. The room was big and full, eight to 10 people per round table, maybe 50 tables. He stood to one side of the elevated stage that ran the width of the room. Of course, two imposing screens, one on each end of the stage, were unfurled like white flags waiting to be emblazoned. And then they were, with slide after illegible slide. If I had taken and passed a speed reading course, I wouldn't have gotten through the slides. There were charts and diagrams and bullet points and excerpts and quotes and flowing things and arrows and go this way and back, and that way and hey, now lookie here this is important and you really need to get this, and while you're at it remember this because see these famous guys said it was so, and now we'll go on to the next slide and I do hope you're really getting all this and remembering it and integrating it into your consciousness and connecting it to your experience and frame of reference and oops, I think I need to go back one or two, and now let's jump ahead to something you'll really like and be able to use — if you're still breathing and conscious.

I wasn't. I was spun into a coma, in which I suffered an acute inner asthma attack that almost killed me. I had my first-ever migraine, and I think somewhere in there I was praying to be taken back to the Mother Ship.

When his talk was mercifully over, he invited me to have a drink with him in the lounge. We sat down at a small round table and ordered drinks. I had only just met him a few minutes before his talk, mind you. He asked, "So, what did you think?" I was silent, weighing several options. He said, "It's OK, I want you to tell me the truth. I want to know what you think."

I was waiting for that invitation. I said something like, "I really enjoyed that bit when you spoke about your values, and why you do what you do. I thought that was very revealing and refreshing. It lasted for about 30 seconds, and it came at the 42-minute mark. By my reckoning, you had 30 seconds of authenticity in a 70 minute talk." I said a bit more. Then I was silent. So was he. Then he said, "I don't like you. And I don't like what you just said."

"I get that a lot."

"*Wait.* Listen to me. I know that I need to hear you. I know that you are right."

I wasn't trying to be right. I was just expressing my point of view. I told him I thought he was hiding behind his slides and information. I asked him why he didn't show up as a human being and say, "Here I am. Please see me. Please hear me. This is who I am and this is what I stand for."

He said he wanted to work with me. I didn't follow up and I never heard from him.

If you're going to be a tour guide for a PowerPoint presentation stay home. If you're just going to point people don't need you.

In business presentations, so much of our speaking is really our hiding. We say the words like a news reader, we withhold ourself behind a neutral mask, speaking neutered words. This isn't speaking. This isn't communicating. This isn't connecting. Giving out information, reading a script, pointing to slides — these are not speaking, not communicating, any more than random pressure on one's inner ear is music.

This "information obsession" is the mindset that creates biz-speak, an information-bearing syntax for androids. "We want to unlock the performance potential for achievement of our most important asset, our human capital."

"Together we can move forward with confidence in the future."

"Apologies for any inconvenience caused."

"There is nothing I can do. It's just our policy."

Translations: No one is here. We're all dead. Have a nice day.

I have a strong opinion about this. I admit my bias for communication first, information second. I do appreciate the value of information, especially information carefully gathered and clearly presented. It's important, in some cases it's vital.

It's just that information doesn't have flesh, or feeling, or humor or empathy. It doesn't love. Information doesn't love, because it doesn't have a soul. People have these things. Where are the people?

It was wonderful to see Lynn come to these realizations in the workshop. It was even more wonderful to see her emerge from behind the hiding place of information and presentation, to stand in her own integrity, to show herself, to share herself, and to enjoy doing it.

Choosing Confidence

Nicole Lloyd

It was about a month before my first of three introductory sessions where I would be speaking in front of small groups of people about my new business: teaching people piano in the Simply Music method. I was advertising in local papers and magazines and people were ringing, inquiring and booking in (to my shock and horror!) to hear all about this "breakthrough piano method." I was doing all the "right" things. I was listening to the training material provided by the company and rehearsing what I was supposed to say as I went on my daily walks around the block. As I was rehearsing, I became more and more nervous. I kept forgetting what I was supposed to talk about. Fear set in. What if I forget what to say on the day? What if people laugh at me or walk out? What if I don't get any students?

Then one fine morning I received an email about the Speak Truthfully course. I had a quick read and booked in straight away. I *knew* I had to do it no matter how shit-scared I was. If I could get through a course like this I could do anything! I rang Robert and clearly remember him saying that the course would be transformational for me. Yes. This is what I wanted – to transform all of those beliefs about myself that prevented me from standing on my own two feet and speaking up! Maybe Robert would be able to help. I was determined, desperate, excited and totally scared out of my brain! Me on video! Speaking! I don't even like seeing myself on video when I'm *not* speaking! What was I getting myself into!

We were given a pre-workshop assignment to be prepared to talk about what's at stake to be better speakers and how important it is for us to be able to speak with authenticity, confidence, and integrity with anyone at anytime. Oh my God. This is so important to me. I looked back through my life and realized all the ways I have avoided speaking the truth and how that has affected the choices I've made, the people I've attracted into my life — really, my whole being. No wonder I've felt a constant lull of depression: I've been depressing my truth, my creative energy, my Self all my life! I thought it was just me, my personality, and that I would have to live with the pain forever. If doing this course could help me be free of this state of being I'll do it with all my heart and soul, no matter how scared I was!

The first day of the workshop arrived. Free from my two beautiful young daughters, Oceana and Amara, for the day! Doing something that nourishes and nurtures my soul. Feeling nervous. Met Robert. Chose a chair to sit in. Met the others in the group. Waited. Joined in the conversation. Laughed a little. I was ready. Surrendered to what the day was to bring. Then after Robert's introduction he asked us to take turns introducing ourselves and talking about why we're here, what's at stake, etc. I took out my notes and realized no one else had any and we actually had to make it up as we went along! My worst nightmare coming true! Make it up! I can't do that! What if I get it wrong? What if I miss out something I wanted to say? What if I go blank like I have in public speaking situations in the past?

I put the notes away. A few people had their turns. I listened while feeling a huge wave of sadness come over me. I realized how sad it was that I had never felt safe to speak up and how so many other people have been stuck and are still stuck in the same way. The tears couldn't help but pour out. I had no tissues so Robert very kindly gave me his green handkerchief, which he didn't want back for some reason. I kept crying. It was my turn — last as usual. I didn't want my tears to get in the way of saying what I wanted to share with the group. I couldn't speak. My throat felt constricted. Robert encouraged me to speak when I was ready. I took a few breaths and managed to talk through the tears about how I've always avoided connecting and speaking with others in an authentic way and how I just don't want to be that way anymore. I sat down. I kept crying. The tap wouldn't turn off. Robert's presence and compassion allowed me to feel safe being that vulnerable. For the rest of the day and some of the next I cried a lot! I felt scared. I felt uncomfortable. I felt vulnerable. But I knew they were only feelings and I was determined (most of the time) not to give in to them!

We had many opportunities to get up and practice speaking in front of the group over the two days. I went blank every time at least once. In those moments I noticed I had "disappeared." I was either thinking about what I should or could say next or giving myself a hard time about what I had just said or worried about what everyone was thinking about me, etc. I therefore wasn't present anymore with myself or the audience. I was just freaking out and wanting to run out the door. I didn't though. Robert reminded me to breathe, feel the ground, connect with each person in the room and to most importantly *choose confidence*. No one had ever told me before that confidence was a choice! As soon as I did those things the words started to flow once again … until the next flip-out! This was a pattern I was familiar with. Another reason why I kept going blank was because I actually was trying to remember what to say next when practicing speaking about my piano teaching, trying to remember what their teaching materials told me I was supposed to say. Robert picked this up right at the end. He said to me that all I have to do is speak from my own experience — not someone else's. That is the only way to speak authentically and therefore the only way an audience will connect with and believe you. I felt a great relief. You mean my own words would be enough? He also said that doubt is all that was in my way. Everything became clear. If I didn't believe any of those thoughts that doubt myself I would be free to speak my truth! If I chose confidence over doubt I wouldn't be "stuck" anymore. This realization became clearer and clearer over the weeks after the course. I thanked Robert, feeling so grateful, honored, and empowered.

For the rest of the week leading up to my first introductory session, I didn't practice anything. I wrote a few points that would help me keep on track — but that's all! I felt a sense of great anticipation, excitement and aliveness. I actually felt a hunger to connect with these people who were coming to meet me for the first time. I couldn't wait to express my passion about learning to play the piano.

The day came. Half an hour before I sat in the piano room, oils burning, heater on, soft music playing, everything in order, heart beating, feet on the ground. I sat in silence watching the trees moving in the wind and rain, feeling peaceful and surprisingly confident! Four people arrived. I greeted them and started speaking. My voice slightly on the quiet side at first but then gradually became more confident and strong. I spoke about my own experience and the words flowed out in their own perfect way. I did know what to say! A few of the people could relate to what I was saying and they all seemed to be interested! In the end they *all* signed up to be my first official piano students! How easy was that! I rang Robert straight away to tell him the great news. He said I should be extremely proud of myself and to go out and celebrate, so I took the family out to Sizzlers. I had two more Introductory Sessions over the next two weeks. Another nine people signed up and I have been enjoying teaching them all for the last two weeks.

Since then I have felt more and more comfortable being grounded, present, confident and authentic. I see clearly that being confident is a choice. I used to be a person consumed in doubt. Doubt is now moving out as confidence and presence are making themselves at home. I am alive. I am big. I am creative. My heart is open. Doubt still makes itself known but I know now what is true and that I have choices. I know that the universe is on my side and all I need to do is trust each and every moment knowing that all the words and wisdom will arise from within when I am still. What I learned is flowing into all aspects of my life. The way I speak and connect with my children, students, friends, family and my husband. I choose confidence when writing, drawing, improvising on the piano (which I have always wanted to do). I am now creating a new, beautiful, creative, authentic life for myself —

with confidence.

I feel so grateful to Robert for emanating confidence and authenticity. He helped me see that I am confident when I choose to be. It has always been there waiting, ready to express Nicole into the world. Doubt was in the way. That was all. Thank you, Robert, for noticing.

Commentary

"Our doubts are traitors, and make us lose the good we oft might win, by fearing to attempt."
William Shakespeare

During the workshop, I was afraid Nicole would fall over from dehydration — she did cry pretty much nonstop! She was, as she says in her essay, shit-scared. She would get up to speak, and then blank out. When she hit this familiar wall she'd start to cry and want to sit down.

I wouldn't let her. I asked her to just stand there, even with her blank mind, streaming tears, and pounding heart. I was firm. I was also empathetic; I know what that terror feels like.

Nicole, stay there. Don't sit down. Just stand there. It's all right. If you want to change your life, if you want to break the pattern, just stand there. Stay in the game! Don't sit down. Breathe. Breathe. Just stand there. Don't worry. You don't have to say anything, you just have to wait out the storm of self-doubt! Breathe. Look around, look here, look at me, look at the others. We are your friends. We are not judging you. We are not criticizing you. We are here to see you and to hear you. You take your time. No hurry. Don't try to think up what to say next, just let it come to you. Be OK in the blank mind. It's OK. The next thing will come by itself. You'll see. Just stay up there.

She did. She never sat down once. She hit the same wall every time up, and she never sat down. She stayed in the game. She was fighting for, and finally chose, a new way to be. She chose confidence over doubt, courage over fear, determination over habit. Right there in front of our eyes, Nicole re-invented herself. She was a master class in courage. She was the purest picture of vulnerability you could imagine. She called up and faced down every demon of self-doubt, every thought of *I'm no good*, every feeling of *I'm crap*.

She blew us all away, because she went into her self-made chrysalis as a caterpillar, and she came out a butterfly, right there in front of us. Over two days. We saw the whole thing.

In the workshops, we spend a fair bit of time on this idea of choosing confidence. As public speakers, we must be credible, which means people must quickly believe that we are going to be straight with them, that we are going to tell them the truth as we know it. In a word, we've got to be real. In all speaking situations, *we* are the message: *we* command attention and respect, *we* inspire others, *we* make the impact. If people do not believe *us*, they will not believe what we say.

Without confidence, we cannot be credible. No one wants to listen to a timid, tentative speaker. In public speaking, a lack of confidence will always undermine our credibility. There are two kinds of confidence: one is earned, one is innate. Earned confidence comes from education and training, or from years of experience. Innate confidence is an attitude of mind, a choice to be fearlessly expressive independent of other factors. Innate confidence is a self-blessing to speak our truth at all times because *I am entitled to speak and to be heard.*

Innate confidence is you being you, when you stop being who you think you should be. This confidence is your voice, when you stop imitating others. This confidence is what you want to say, when you stop trying to please others. This confidence is purely you, no one else. Confidence tells you to look for cliffs to jump from — knowing you will build your wings on the way down!

This confidence is our innate right to stand up and speak our truth with passion, tenderness, and full freedom. This confidence says: *I belong here. I have a place here. I am entitled to speak and to be heard.*

Nicole is choosing this kind of confidence!

I'd like to share with you part of the email exchange I had with Nicole about her essay. After reading her piece, I wrote:

Dear Nicole: I just read your essay. It is brilliant. I have published five books and more than 250 articles, and I don't think I've ever written something so truthful, moving, and beautiful.

To which she replied, via email:

Hi Robert: Brilliant??????? That's the first time anyone has ever said something I have written is brilliant. But I can see that's because I've never written an essay from my heart, only what I thought the teacher wanted me to write — which is why it was always such a struggle. Thank you for giving me the opportunity to write what I wrote. It has been wanting to come out of me.

So many things within us want to come out. Life does not hide; it's on display all the time. When we choose confidence, our whole being shudders awake with all these things that want to come out!

Nicole has taken a couple more workshops since the first one about which she writes in her essay. In one talk, I asked her to be Mrs. King Kong. I asked her to scold Mr. Kong, who had come in late from a night of carousing with his monkey mates. I asked her to really go for it. She did.

Mr. Kong was put right in his place, thank you very much. Nicole got a taste of her own fierceness, her own bigness. I believe she's making a new life for herself, as Mrs. Kong!

As Professor Dumbledore said in *Harry Potter and the Chamber of*

Secrets: “It is our choices, Harry, that show what we are, far more than our abilities.” Nicole chooses confidence.

Dark Night Of The Soul

Margaret Gill

Only a short six months before this hideous "dark night of the soul," I had been safe, in a place of power, earning good money, and walking the corridors of influence in large corporations. Now lying on the icy cold floor of my un-insulated 100-year-old Victorian home as the temperature outside dropped precariously close to zero, I heard an internal piercing scream as I felt the dream in my heart shatter. At that precise moment in time my entire being froze physically, mentally, and spiritually.

Hours of sobbing had left me too exhausted to drag myself up off the floor but now as the darkness and freezing cold penetrated my senses, I had not one single tear left in my body to weep. This was rock bottom and I had hit it hard.

The decision to become a corporate refugee was easy. The reality of the change turned into a living nightmare.

It was meant to be easy; all the self-help books had said, "follow your dream and the path will open before you." In six months the only path I had managed to find was the one that ended in a dole queue. As I lay there on the floor having had my newfound title of dole-bludger stamped on my forehead earlier that day, the story of the last six months resounded in my head like a long-playing record stuck in a groove.

Over and over I chastised myself for being so stupid. Where was my head to think I could move to a small country town and succeed where I only knew two people? How could I have thought I could set up a new small business, unsupported, in an area I knew nothing about after only having contracted within the safety net of big organizations for the last ten years? To tell people I had been possessed by aliens would have given me more personal credibility than the truth that was currently unfolding. I had seriously messed up and the rainy day pool was now drier than a drought-stricken landscape. What's more, the bank was coming after my house. This wasn't how it was meant to play out, and the shame and belief that I was a big fat loser stopped me from asking for the help of caring family and friends.

The situation I found myself in was only a symptom of the core issue. The real problem was that I was shy and I had no networking experience. I'd spent the past few years resolving problems with IT geeks and accountants where, in retrospect, my introverted personality had found a safe and quiet home. But now that I had traded in that safety for the adventure of my dream,

I realized, as did others, that I'd have to speak in public to get the recognition I needed to make the dream work. Didn't they know given the choice I'd rather fall face first into a vat of cold vomit than get up in front of any audience to speak publicly?

But at sometime during that dark night of the soul, my dream re-ignited and a small shaky voice in my heart started to plead with me to *get up, get up, get up*. It just kept repeating in my head until finally I managed to find the strength somewhere within to pull myself onto the bed and pull the covers over my head. I had pulled myself off rock bottom but was still hanging by a very loose emotional thread.

What I realize now is that my fear of public speaking was the biggest contributing factor to the situation I found myself in at that time. I couldn't even speak one-on-one with people, let alone walk into a big room full of strangers and network or (worse still!) get up on a stage and speak. As it turned out, the dream to get out of the corporate world and work positively with people was bigger than the fear. I finally put my hand up to speak at a small local event. To say I bombed would have been the kindest way to describe the experience, actually it was a total disaster and I left feeling like a deflated balloon. Sadly it was not my only bad experience and I truly wish I had found Speak Truthfully about three years before I did.

I first encountered Robert when he was in Australia on a speaking tour. I was really impressed with the way he could sit and say nothing and keep a room full of people transfixed in the palm of his hand. He told me later he superglues the chairs; no, seriously, it was his gift of remaining so present that he didn't have to say anything which fascinated me. When I found out he had moved to Australia and was offering Speak Truthfully classes to help people sell themselves as the product, I jumped at the chance to get in the queue for a place on the course. Finally I'd found a path that enhanced my dream.

By the time I did the workshop, I had done quite a bit of public speaking and even a couple of appearances on current affairs shows speaking about the dark side of sea change, something I had come to know a lot about. During these experiences people had started to give me feedback like "you speak from the heart," "you are a natural," and "your story inspired me" but I kept thinking *oh, they are just being kind* or more likely just pissing in my pocket. I couldn't find a place in any of my cells that could accept those compliments, as much as I needed to and as much as I tried.

The thing I got the most out of during the Speak Truthfully course was the videotaping and playback of our speaking. I had never had the opportunity to sit and watch myself. I had videos of my TV appearances, which I was too scared to watch for fear of seeing what I felt must have been me making a complete twat of myself on national TV. Robert gave me no option but to sit there and watch. I thought I had done quite well just to do that; but then he made me speak about what I saw, he asked me to evaluate my own speaking! This whole process made me feel really uncomfortable inside. It took me quite a few takes before I could start to see what people had been telling me and then verbalize it. Finally, I could see the warmth in who I was and I could see why people wanted to listen to my story. There it was, the undeniable truth: I did have something to say! What's more, others thought so as well. This released me from a whole lot of personal fear and really opened my world up, quite literally. My free 90 Day Challenge online product offering for holistic and natural therapists has started to be picked up and used in other countries, and now I would have the confidence to go and speak to people in other countries, from my heart.

It was wonderful to see others go through the same process, and I think being part of a group really helped. It was quite revealing to see someone doing really well, but then hear them bag themselves. I could see *my* fears playing out in *their* actions, and it was reassuring to know that even though they thought they were doing badly, they had something really interesting to say or were connecting at a deep level or they were funny. Recalling a tall reserved lawyer doing a Fozzie Bear routine will always return a smile. Being with people who were prepared to bare their souls made it really easy to learn at many different levels.

The course has also helped me have more meaningful conversations with others. Before Speak Truthfully, I found it difficult to talk to strangers about what I do. Actually, let's be honest, I had trouble talking with strangers, full stop! I now have the confidence to go to the "now" moment and stay in that place and keep myself centered and focused on what I am saying. I no longer spend time looking for the door. This new capacity has helped my business on many levels and has helped me grow as a person.

I have continued to speak more in public and actually find I enjoy connecting with others now. My knees still knock and I always spend the hour before wondering why on earth I agreed to do the gig. But once up there and started I only have to take myself back to that place in class when I first saw what others see and I can continue in confidence knowing "I'm all right." In fact it's a little more than that — I'm a remarkable dream in progress. Thanks, Robert, for helping me make the dream come closer.

Commentary

"Nobody can be alive for you. Nor can you be alive for anyone else."
e.e. cummings

Margaret's phrase "belief that I was a big fat loser" makes it pretty easy for me to select the theme for this Commentary: the inner critic!

Nasty aren't they, those little inner critics. I've never met anyone who doesn't have at least one. I used to have so many critics in my head that they banded together in what I called police forces, and they worked day and night to keep my authenticity under house arrest. There was a time when almost anything I said, or wanted to say, would arouse the attention of one or another of these internal police forces who would turn on their sirens and flash their lights. Booming in my head, I would hear them bellow, "Hey, pull over. Right now! Who do you think you are? You are speaking without permission, without a license. Who told you that you could speak like that? Stop that right now. You are just crap. You were always crap and you'll always be crap. You are under arrest!"

These critics and police forces live somewhere within us, waiting to pounce on what we want to say or do, ready to rip us apart as being not good enough, in some way or another. In the eyes of the critics, or police, we are guilty, even if proven innocent! Condemned to an eternity of cowering, because you are a big fat loser!

Where do these speaking critics and idea police come from? We spend a fair bit of time with this question in the workshop. It is quite important that we realize for ourselves that we are the creators of the critics, we energize them, we give and maintain their life and their force in our lives. Once we see this, we can then use the very same shakti that we use to keep the critics in place to banish them to oblivion. This is how we use our shakti to choose confidence.

I'd like you to spend some time now, working with these ideas in the way we do in the Speak Truthfully workshop.

Following is the exercise I use to help people discover the origin of their critics and police forces. Play around with it; see what you come up with. See if you can find some ways that you are living in speaking poverty because of an earlier decision you made. And then enrich your speaking and your life with new choices, ones of desert-like quietness, brewing storms, and self-authored authenticity! Remember, it's not who you are that holds you back, it's who you think you're not!

Speaking Truthfully Fear

It is not natural to be afraid of speaking truthfully; it is a self-inflicted wound. Many of us have had negative experiences around our self-expression, after which we made self-limiting decisions about the safety of fully and authentically speaking our inner truth, thinking it not safe to do so. Perhaps we were criticized, rejected, embarrassed, or denounced by people with more power and authority than we had at that time. These self-limiting decisions about our worthiness to stand and speak our truth become fearful beliefs, which undermine our capacity to speak with confidence and self-acceptance. We can dissolve these fearful beliefs anytime we want, because they exist within us through our own power. They have no independent power.

Take a few minutes to reflect on any such negative experiences you might have had, and how you made self-limiting decisions that became your fearful beliefs about public speaking. Use the chart below to summarize your reflections.

Experience	*Limiting Decision*	*Fearful Belief*

Recovering My Voice

Michelle Wilson

I first met Robert when my husband, Adam, and I went to his "Communicating in Intimate Relationships" workshop that he was holding in Melbourne. My husband needed to coax me to go, because I was apprehensive about what I might have been asked to do. The thought of having to participate and share my thoughts was daunting for me. I really wanted to go because I knew that I would benefit and learn a lot. Still, I was nervous.

I've always been really confident when it comes to being an osteopath, but outside of work I didn't have the same confidence. I found it easier and safer to stay quiet and just agree with others rather than voicing my own thoughts. I was always concerned about what others would think of me. I didn't like the thought of being judged and criticized. Therefore, I found it hard to express my emotions and feelings and didn't do it very often. I actually really feared it because I felt it would lead to confrontation. This meant that any situation with someone where I felt my voice might be judged, I kept quiet. I didn't have enough confidence and belief in myself to be able to deal with other people's reactions, especially if it meant there was any chance they may not agree with what I said. I found any conversation that meant I had to stand up for my opinion as confrontational.

When I met Robert and heard him speak, I thought he was not only the best speaker I had heard, but he had the most warming, calming, passionate, and funny personality. He was so honest in his words and was able to put things in perspective so easily. Adam and I were sufficiently inspired that we booked in for the Speak Truthfully course right after this workshop, even though I knew I would have to stand up and speak! If I thought I was anxious before the communication workshop, you should have seen what was happening in my mind before the Speak Truthfully course! I told Robert that I had so much fear about speaking and sharing my ideas in front of others; he laughed and said not to worry. He said to bring along my fears and doubts to the course, and he wouldn't even charge me extra. They could come for free!

They were certainly alongside me when I walked in on the first day. I wasn't at all confident to stand up and speak in front of people even if it was only a small group. The fear of being judged and criticized for what I said and thought came creeping into my mind. I didn't feel that I had anything of interest to share with the group. I was extremely nervous about self-expression because I never felt comfortable talking about myself. It started to become clear how low my self-esteem had become. As we talked and worked through course topics like "authenticity" and "confidence," I realized that I didn't value my own beliefs at all. I had been living my life doubting myself so much that I would always think someone else's beliefs and opinions were right — even if I didn't agree.

I learned and realized so many things in the Speak Truthfully course that helped me transform my fears and doubts. While growing up I had listened to people who always seemed to sound so negative and overly dramatic when talking about themselves, which was a turn off for me. This lead me to think that when you talk about yourself no one would want to listen. I thought this way all my life, that to talk about yourself would turn people off, so I didn't talk about myself or what I thought and felt. Because I wouldn't express myself, I developed a very doubtful and low opinion of myself. Throughout the workshop it became clear that I was living my life mostly to make other people happy, trying to make sure that I was as nice to everyone as I could. This meant I never had to rock the boat with anyone and I could stay out of everyone's way.

The thing I realized was this: I was not living my own life. I was not being true to myself and I was certainly not speaking with *my* voice. I asked myself what kind of life was I living by letting other people be my voice. I suddenly had the need to speak my own opinion and to value *my* opinions as important and true, because they were mine. I realized that my thoughts and feelings and values are not wrong, because they are what I believe. I am my own person and I will certainly have my own opinions which I am entitled to, even if they are different from others. By speaking my own voice and being true to myself, I felt much more alive and happy. That feeling of always holding back and suppressing my thoughts and feelings, which had made me feel sick and nervous, has gone.

Throughout the workshop, the images of children, especially of my beautiful niece and nephew, came up a lot. The fact that children are so happy and honest all the time. They always speak their own voice and tell things as they see it. As we get older I think we lose the ability to have that same honesty and speak our own voice. I feel that everyone can learn a lot from children also.

Through the course I found the confidence within myself that was always there, but that I had lost touch with. By speaking the truth from my heart, I found it easy to get up and talk in front of people. Perfect timing for that to happen, because a few months later, when I got up to give my wedding speech, I was able to enjoy giving it. It was easy instead of terrifying. I could really be present with myself and others on that special day, and in that moment I could express my feelings of love.

I now know that I have so much to offer to people and my thoughts and opinions are a part of me and "my" voice. Why would I hide behind someone else's thoughts? They aren't living my life; I am. Life is fantastic when "I" am the message that I want to send to people. I previously worried too much about what others thought about me and was not true to myself and did not speak with my own voice. I now say, "Be true to yourself, speak out loud, and let your voice be heard. You will never turn back!"

Commentary

"If I didn't define myself for myself, I would be crunched into other people's fantasies for me and eaten alive."
Audre Lorde

A couple of days after Michelle's workshop, I received a card from her, in which she had written:

Dear Robert,
Thank you for such a wonderful day on Sunday. Thank you for showing me that speaking out loud about myself doesn't have to be associated with negativity. I wanted you to know that although I didn't get up and say a taboo word, I did say mine earlier. I have never once volunteered that I had anorexia to anyone that doesn't know me. I can never bring myself to say it. I realize it is partly because I am embarrassed about it because most people thought I did it to get attention. Attention was truly the last thing I wanted at that time. I can see my self-worth and confidence was so low I didn't even think I deserved food!!
Thanks again,
Michelle

The "taboo" Michelle mentions refers to a speaking exercise I sometimes invite people to do. From early in our adventure on planet Earth, we are told there are certain things that we just cannot say. We are told that certain words, ideas, or phrases are inherently bad, or taboo. We may have been told to keep secret things that happened, or were done to us. Shame, embarrassment, intimidation, and fear have created a storehouse of taboos.

These taboos, these locked doors, keep us from our authenticity, our freedom, our energy, our poetry, our endless creative possibilities. We live in the small cramped space that taboos grant us, even though we may not know we have them, or remember from where they came.

Speak Truthfully is about freedom of self-expression. In order to speak our most authentic and daring ideas and feelings, we have to be able to say anything. Yes, of course, we want our freedom to be effective, not just wild and random raving. But to make speaking choices, to decide what to say and how to say it, requires freedom. If we are not free to choose, because of fear of saying certain things, then our fear, not us, chooses what we can say.

Philip Pullman, the author of a sophisticated trilogy of children's novels called, collectively, *His Dark Materials*, has a pertinent memory from his final year in school. He and his friend Merfyn Jones represented their school in a debate against a team from the local private girls' school. "We basically were defending anarchy," he recalled. "People couldn't quite believe what we were saying, that we were saying it in quite this way, and that we were using quotes from various poets and politicians." Afterward, Pullman said, some girls from the other school came up to the teen-age firebrands and asked, "How are you allowed to say these things? We're not even allowed to think about thinking about these things!"

In the taboo exercise, I ask people to identify any taboos — thoughts, words, or events — they are afraid to speak, things they've been told they *just cannot say*. It is often an incendiary report that follows. I've talked it over with myself, debating whether or not to publish some of the things people have said. I've decided to not print them, and for this reason: the exercise is less about what they say, then their process of reclaiming their sovereignty over their own creative self-expression. The value of the exercise is in their reclaiming their own power to speak what ever they may want to say, and from that place of freedom and self-determination decide what they want to say.

You can work with this right now. Make a list of taboos. Be honest with yourself. Don't censor, just write. When you're done, see if you want to say what you've written out loud, just to yourself, maybe to a trusted partner or friend. See what happens when you free up the energy you suppressed, you buried along with the taboo. You can only be free to not say something if you first can say it. And, if you succumb to a taboo, you harm the soul of authentic self-expression, of speaking truthfully.

Remaining Present

Adam Wilson

I first met Robert in 2006 at a workshop he was presenting in Melbourne, and was amazed by his honesty and openness. We spoke for a while after the workshop about various things, and l found out a little about his upcoming Speak Truthfully course. I was intrigued by Robert in our early discussions. I wanted to spend more time with him so I could learn from him. The Speak Truthfully workshop offered me a great chance to do that.

As an osteopath, I have been taught so many wonderful things about the body. I have studied subjects including anatomy, physiology, biochemistry, neuroanatomy, and psychology. I was also taught hundreds of fantastic techniques designed to resolve all sorts of muscular aches and pains. The one thing that was lacking in our training was how to communicate effectively. In our five years of study I never felt like I developed any skills that may help relate and truly connect with my patients. The ability to listen and effectively communicate with people is *the* most important aspect of my job, and it was a skill that I was lacking.

I had never really paid too much attention to this very important fact. I always thought things were going along fine. It wasn't until about two years ago, when I began noticing some real limitations with my work that the importance of effective communication became obvious. I was finding it very difficult to maintain focus, and my mind was constantly wandering. I was getting bored, and work was becoming a burden. I was slowly losing my motivation and passion for being an osteopath. Like many people who have participated in Robert's workshop, I had already begun my own personal journey to seek my truth. I had read many books and participated in other workshops, but nothing compares to the experiences I shared during the two days at this workshop. What became crystal clear to me during those two days was that my lack of focus, increasing boredom, and inability to stay focused all came from the same source: my inability to stay present. I had been spending so much time and energy thinking about how things were going to be in the future, that my attention had been completely taken away from what was happening right now!

Robert's course has taught me about genuine self-expression and opened the door to a new way of life. There is no urgency in my life anymore. I no longer concern myself with what may be. If I am present, I will always be listening. If I can remain present, I will always speak my truth.

Since participating in Robert's course nearly twelve months ago, my life has constantly changed. My boredom, and lack of focus at work has been replaced with excitement and complete devotion. The feelings of frustration and impatience have been replaced by stillness and a deep sense of calm.

There is nothing else in the world that I would rather be doing other than what I am doing right now.

Commentary

"We are here and it is now. Further than that all human knowledge is moonshine."
H. L. Mencken

Being Present. Awareness. Listening. Authenticity. Truth. Confidence. One follows on from the other, and leads back again. Of course we have to be present in our speaking. We have to be present in our life.

I want to offer a caution about this notion of being present, which Adam speaks of. It can be very cathartic, explosive, and transformative. It can rock our boat! Being present means to pay close attention to what we are saying, and also to the truth of it. Someone recently asked me, "Can we speak authentically if we aren't telling the truth?" I let her answer for herself.

In my workshops, I talk about authentic connection. People hear it at a level and in a way that is appropriate to them, at that time. I invite people to stand and show themselves, share their truth, be bold and unafraid of criticism and judgment. I ask the workshop participants to join me in creating an environment of appreciative listening and respect for the speaker. I say that sometimes a speaker may want to rip the lid off of years of suppression, or anger, or resentment. I say that sometimes a speaker may want to say shocking, wild, crazy things. One never knows. I ask people to be friendly and tolerant and supportive, so that the speaker can use our goodwill and appreciative listening as energy, fuel, or wind for where they might want to go. As you read on, remember: I teach public speaking. I talk about authenticity. OK, yes, I define public speaking as "how we move in and through life," so speaking is more than just using our mouth on a stage. However, I am not a career counselor or life coach. I am not a therapist. I don't know what people should do. I don't focus on their life or career issues. I just teach speaking truthfully.

Nonetheless — one woman, in the late morning of the first day, stood up to talk. I don't remember what her topic was. It didn't matter. Something else happened. She was quiet for a while, practicing the principles I had taught: breathing, grounding, gathering, and connecting. Then she began: "I think I understand what this authenticity is all about. It's not just an idea for speaking. It's a commitment to a way of living. How can I speak to you authentically, when so much of my life is a lie." A long silence. "I think I need to go home tonight and tell my husband I've been having an affair for three years."

In another workshop, a middle-aged corporate manager in the mental health industry sat quietly for most of the first day. He had retreated somewhat into himself, which can happen. The tone of his talks was quite somber, as he was. I felt he was processing something important, and I let him alone. I was standing in front of the group, saying something or another, when this quiet man said softly from his chair, "I know why I'm so unhappy. I hate my job. I quit."

In almost every workshop, someone experiences this kind of life-altering epiphany.

One woman told us that she wanted to gain confidence for an upcoming job interview. She was a school teacher, who had applied for a job in the school system's administration. She had an oral presentation in the coming week, was practicing her comments, and responded to our "question." As she talked, she seemed to me to be going through the motions. She didn't speak with any conviction, or energy. I asked her about that. She said she would bring more shakti. But talk after talk, she remained flat. On the second day, she got up to speak. She stood for a long time, really settling into herself, becoming present and aware of herself. She began speaking, "I've been thinking overnight about why I can't seem to muster the energy and enthusiasm you want to see from me. It's because I don't really want the job. In fact, I don't even like teaching. I don't want to teach. I want to quit. I want to open a catering business with my partner."

What do you think? Can we speak authentically if we aren't telling the truth?

Speaking Truthfully is an amazing adventure. It seems to call us out of complacency and habit and boredom. It seems to wake us up. Authenticity in speaking is not a technique. It can't be faked. And from what people tell me, they don't want to fake it. Sometimes they will say things that are unsafe, just to force the issue, to get their life back from inattention and laziness. You know what I mean?

Undoing The Past

Ida Lyall

I was born in Serbia, the former Yugoslavia, of Hungarian parents. The northern part of Serbia was a melting pot of cultures, religions, and customs. It was called the breadbasket of the country. I had a happy childhood there. After high school I went into civil engineering. My passion was to help people in some way, but I was not very clear on how to do that. I reasoned that building bridges and roads helps people, their lifestyle and comfort.

In university, when I was twenty, I had a synchronistic meeting with my first spiritual teacher. He talked about the meaning of life and death, and the mysteries of illness and healing. It was fascinating to listen and learn about the greater dimensions of life. This encounter was the first seed that Life planted in me, which later blossomed as my work today as a holistic healer.

After WWII, my aunt came to Australia. She invited me to move here, which I did because I wanted to see the world with my own eyes. Even though most people thought I was crazy, I came to Australia with only $20 and 50 words of English. I told the doubting family and friends that I had an adventurous spirit. Within three months of my arrival, my aunt died. I found myself virtually homeless and without means in a country whose language I couldn't speak!

Still, I persevered, and soon got a job in a civil engineering company, where I worked for 27 years. I met my husband there and we were married for 20 years.

Shortly after I began work in engineering and for the next 20 years, I experienced poor health, digestive problems, chronic lower back pain, migraines, and muscle ache. I went to all the available medical resources at the time, but no one could figure out what was wrong. By early 1990, the pain was becoming unbearable and I had to do something. So, I was led to a naturopath, a chiropractor, and a dentist. I experienced physical relief. And then my husband was diagnosed with cancer.

My own healing was put on the back burner. I focused on helping my husband. I looked into alternative or complimentary modalities. During my search for health and healing advice for my husband, I realized the importance of the person's state of mind. I realized that our state of mind is the key to our state of health.

Then, from one of my teachers, I learned the following, "There can be no true healing without an internal shift in attitude and belief." These words struck me in my core, and in a flash I realized that I had to find out about the full and deep meaning of this statement. I realized that I had to learn how to change attitudes and beliefs. The subject became my passion and as a result of that passion, I became a holistic healer.

After seven years of healing and teaching people the time had come to broaden my horizon and reach a wider audience with my message. This is when I was invited to give a TV interview. I panicked. *I cannot communicate to a large audience*, I said to myself. *I cannot express myself clearly*. It was too daunting for me to be seen by so many people and for my words to be heard. My desire to broaden my horizon hit the wall of my fear to do that. I felt small and inadequate. The TV interview had stirred up all kinds of fears and limitations of self-expression. I was finding all kinds of excuses, including that English was my third language so how could I be expected to communicate well!

During this time of my inner battles, Robert came to live in Melbourne. I attended a number of his workshops, even hosting a couple in my home. I instinctively knew that his manner of speaking was what I was looking for, what I wanted to be able to do. He was communicating the way I felt inside, and demonstrated how I would like to do it. I also knew that he was the person who could help me.

I took his Speak Truthfully courses, but I felt I needed personal work, so we started work soon after. I wanted his help to prepare the answers to the questions I knew I would be asked, and to help me get ready to face down my fears of speaking to a big audience. After we had sketched out the points and stories I would use as responses, I began to practice. I would try hard to memorize the text as I prepared for our sessions, just as I had done in the past when needing to present in my workshops and training programs.

Robert trained his camera on me and we pretended to be in the TV studio. He asked me questions and I would give my prepared, rehearsed answers as best I could although I would often lose my place. With all my effort and energy going to "remembering" what I was supposed to say, I could not project my voice. I was not looking at or connecting with the interviewer. I was nervous and uneasy, feeling that my story was not interesting or worthy to be told. I was so busy remembering the text that I could not concentrate on anything else.

Robert kept pointing out, in a compassionate manner, everything I did not do right. He suggested that I stop trying to remember the scripted answers and speak more spontaneously. After all, he said, everything I had to say was what I knew well, including my own life story! In his philosophy of public speaking, the most important aspect is to be fully present and connected with oneself and the audience. I couldn't be present or connected if I was trying to remember what was in my memory.

But I could not do what I was asked to do. I simply could not abandon the "text." The tears started rolling down my face.

Then a long-forgotten memory surfaced from my childhood. I was eight years old. My teacher had chosen a poem for me to recite by a very well known Hungarian poet, for the upcoming community celebrations. I learned the poem by memory, even though as an eight-year-old, I did not understand the meaning and the complexity of the message of the poem.

The day of the celebration arrived. There was an audience of around 500 people, everybody that I knew from the community. My turn came to perform. I started reciting the poem and then I forgot a line. I stood there in confusion and finally left the stage in defeat.

I felt shame and embarrassment. I felt that I failed my father who helped me learn the poem. I failed my teacher's trust in my abilities and the audience's expectations. I failed the poet who wrote the beautiful words of courage and vision of freedom he had for the Hungarian nation and for the world. Last but not least: I failed myself.

That was my last public performance.

I carried this feeling of failure, shame, and deep wounding from early childhood in my psyche for decades. Without consciously knowing it, I decided to never again risk such profound humiliation. Now, when the opportunity and time came to communicate to the public again, decades later, I could not do it. The past memory of failure was overpowering my present desire.

I realized that my dependency on the script was really about the fear of again losing my place and not knowing what to say. With Robert's help and guidance, I also realized the difference between that eight-year-old girl and who I was now. I was able to dissolve the hold that the memory had on me. I found confidence in speaking in front of a public. As we continued our work, I no longer needed to recite the script, but became able to speak spontaneously and with authenticity and freedom! I reclaimed my voice, power of speaking, and trust in my self. It was a wonderful transformation into wholeness.

To complete the story, the TV interview was a huge success, with people in the studio remarking on my poise and clarity. I even was invited to give a lecture at the Melbourne Theosophical Society, which I did!

Commentary

"Love takes off masks that we fear we cannot live without and know we cannot live within."
James Baldwin

I learn from my students the many subsidiary benefits of speaking truthfully, of speaking from the heart. In Ida's case, she talks about healing from a decades-long wound: "I carried this feeling of failure, shame, and deep wounding from early childhood in my psyche for decades. Without consciously knowing it, I decided to never again risk such profound humiliation." For her, and for others, Speak Truthfully initiates a process of healing inner wounds as they walk a path of authentic self-expression.

It's ingenious, really, how many ways there are to reveal and heal such a wound. In Ida's case, it was her striving for performance perfection that initiated the healing. In our meetings, Ida would come with meticulous scripts, having labored over each word, phrase, sentence, and paragraph. We'd review her work and then move into a "TV interview" mode. I'd point the camera at her and sit at some distance, asking the questions we'd prepared. Ida went into "performance" mode. Even when she managed to say exactly what she had scripted, her presence and connection were lacking. She thought that writing and speaking were the same. They are not. Writing is about perfection; speaking is about connection.

How one speaks is vastly different from how one writes; each has its own syntax and rhythm, each its own magic. Each has its merits; each its advantages and disadvantages. Writing can be honed and sharpened and worked and re-worked until it shines. It's less for the moment and more for posterity. Speaking is less worked and more for the moment, what with the inevitable spontaneity that comes from authentic connection to audience, place, and time. Speaking is full of energy, presence, and connection. A recited written text is not speaking.

Ida and I had worked up a series of questions we knew her interviewer would ask. In between our sessions, Ida was to script her talking points, inventory of illustrative anecdotes and stories, and create the narrative flow and arch of her life story and work.

She did. But when it came time for us to talk on camera, she couldn't leave the prepared script. She wasn't present at all, she was in her mind referencing and reading from the text she had prepared. If she faltered, she'd despair. If she lost her place, she'd become desperate. Mind you, we're talking about an extremely intelligent and accomplished woman, one of Australia's premier holistic healers. And, she was talking about what she knew intimately: her life story and the healing modalities she had mastered. But her wounding wouldn't let her be present. It kept dragging her back in time until she was again standing in shame and failure on that stage that no longer existed, as the little girl she no longer was.

She was determined to "get it right" this time! It was this very attitude that kept swamping her and sabotaging her best efforts, because *I want to get it right* does not belong in public speaking. *I want to get it right* leads to performance, which takes us away from ourselves, out of the moment, away from the audience, and into an internal competition with an ideal, some idol of our own imagining.

Performing pits us against an internalized image of what we have established as "right and good." The unforgiving performance beast, born in the belly of a past decision about our worth, says, "You are not good enough." So, we resort to some kind of performance, some way of being that is not authentic, not real, not present — and all about appeasing the beast. Of course, we never can, because the real issue is not what we say, but who we are. Yes, we may blow or forget a line, stumble here or there. So what? A missing word or blown line is not who we are.

Ida is not alone in trying to perform her way to credibility and acceptance. Most people in my workshop start out performing. It is a refuge of sorts. It is safe back there behind the dance steps painted on the floor to move here just like this and then move there just like that and again, two, three, four. Slowly they emerge. *They* emerge from behind the performance. Authenticity and connection are not performance-based. They are not techniques. We don't want to hide behind a script or performance. We want to get out in front. We can never perform our way to authenticity. We have to be authentic enough to ban and banish the beast of performance.

My Authentic Song

Bianca Pickett

"What is the source of our first suffering? It lies in the fact that we hesitated to speak. It was born in the moment when we accumulated silent things within us."
Gaston Bachelard

Do you wonder why your voice gets stuck in your throat, like a stone, blocking the urge to speak, leaving the discomfort of forced silence in the air? I do.

I have a deep need to speak my truth, a term kindly lent to me from Robert Rabbin and his Speak Truthfully course. Since I was a little girl I have fought the urge to write, to let the words tumble out of my pen, my mouth, in a never ending stream of consciousness, because I feared it would never stop. Why have I limited myself?

Very early on I was heavily scrutinized, judged and criticized for speaking my truth, because it didn't fit into the ideal of the "perfect child" that my mother had attached to me. I was told I was too quiet, too honest, too "painfully shy," too loud, too smart, too everything. I realized at the age of about eight years old, when I took my homework to my mother for help, that I had outgrown my mother's intellectual ability; but it has taken me another 24 years to outgrow her negative power over me.

My family and my history has been tumultuous to say the least, and part of this has been keeping as much of it as secret as possible, so my mother could pretend that it wasn't happening. Appearances were, for some strange reason, very important to her. Looking back now, I think people would have understood and helped us; instead we had to pretend, to lie, to act as if everything was rosy. A childhood of secrets and pretense had created a wall around me that I wasn't aware was there or the extent to which it affected my life, let alone how to get through it to the other side.

I have been searching my whole adult life for answers, for meaning, for purpose, and in my never-ending self-help quest I came upon Robert's books, and then his Speak Truthfully course. I pondered why I booked myself in to his class, as I have no fear of public speaking, but he soon made me realize that the person I was presenting as me, wasn't me, it was a façade, the "appearance of me." What Robert made me realize is that in order to connect with an audience, whether that be one or many, you have to be authentic. The challenge was to find that authentic person on the inside, and then figure out how the hell to present that to the world. Then he asked me to sing.

Singing for me is a private expression of emotion. I have always sung, under my breath, at work, or running in the morning. I sing all the time: it comforts me, it is my constant rhythm of life. I have never been one for fame and adulation, so singing in front of an audience is a rare occurrence. But when Robert asked me to sing in front of his class, rather than speak on a topic of my choice, the fear of death spread through my veins. Why didn't he ask me to talk about my family, my work, books, music, something I am comfortable with — but no. Like the blood hound that he is, he asked me to do the one thing that would tear all the layers of my façade off, and break me down to my authentic *me*. For some strange reason I have a song that I sing all the time, not necessarily for the meaning of the song, I just love the feeling of it. It is "Me and a Gun" by Tori Amos, an unaccompanied song she sings about being raped. I sang this song, and felt the wall crumbling around me, just as I am sure Robert had intuited it would. It is an unbelievably powerful thing to connect with the energy in a room with your self-expression, and move not only yourself to near tears, but those around you.

I take this lesson with me now, and use it every day, in everything I do. I know now what being authentic means, I know what real connection is. It is something I feel I have to be sparring with, and I will forever be learning when and how to use it. But for me the mere understanding of it is a revelation that I will be eternally grateful to Robert for.

Commentary

"Somewhere in a burst of glory, sound becomes song."
Paul Simon

In addition to being an astoundingly competent and compassionate corporate manager, Bianca is dialed into the spirit world; she's a natural healer. She told me that dead grandmothers talk to her, and she was a bit freaked out at that. She didn't know exactly where her gifts of intuitive knowing and powers of healing came from. Neither did I. But in talking together, we made it OK for her to know things, without knowing how; we made it OK for her to come out from her hiding place and "own" her gifts. She dissolved her self-doubts and fed her inner strength. She was nutrient deficient, because, as she says in her essay, she didn't get much support and acknowledgement for her creative spirit and authentic voice when she was growing up — let alone for consorting with senior citizens of the spirit world!

This is a common form of self-suppression: self-doubt as a protective mechanism from the harsh judgments of others. We all know the sting of being put-down, criticized, and yanked out of our wonderment and intuitive imagination. We shut down and go into a kind of hiding from our authentic self — giving birth to the façade she mentioned, the wall behind which we live, unable to speak. We pretend, put on an act, try to fit in, say things that are safe. That seeming safety comes at a cost.

What a beautiful and poignant opening sentence Bianca writes, "Do you wonder why your voice gets stuck in your throat, like a stone, blocking the urge to speak, leaving the discomfort of forced silence in the air?" I wondered about that for years. It felt as if I had another person in me, an inner shadowy self that was too afraid to come out into the light. Many of the people who come to a workshop are trying to figure that out, too. At some point in our life, though, the cost of keeping our voice stuck is too suffocating and it becomes almost a matter of life and death to cough out the stone and start speaking the truth that is within our heart, inviting our shadowy inner being to come out and play.

One of the areas we explore in the workshop is the difference between *then* and *now*, between what we had to do to survive when we were young, vulnerable, and often defenseless against harshness, and what we are able to do *now*. We discover that now we have resources of strength and power we didn't have then. With the discovered strength and power of now, we can write another script, we can start singing and see that not only does no harm come to us, but we begin to experience the authentic self that we knew was always there but wouldn't speak, sing, or shout. It takes a bit of courage to take that first step, to sing that first note, but with a little encouragement, pretty soon we're getting our stuff out there, in our distinctive way. Bianca has that courage, that resolve, because she couldn't keep that stone in her throat any more.

My Aunt's 50th Birthday

John Anderson

For me, the real gift of Speak Truthfully is the knowing that I will never again withhold what's in my heart to say due to a fear of public speaking. The reason for this new certainty is in knowing that I can always get centered within myself, and from that place express my "truth," even if I don't at first say it "perfectly" or with full confidence — if it's from my heart, my message will still resonate with people as the truth, my truth.

A great example of this was at my aunt's 50th birthday. She was very close to me. It was that time of night when it was time for the speeches. We were in a room of more than a hundred people, all of whom had known my aunt for many years, and all of whom loved her very much and doubtless had countless stories about her.

Even so, was there a big flock of people going to the front of the room to express their love for my aunt? No! In fact, the MC, my cousin who organized the event, had to prompt people to get up and come forward to the microphone.

I felt nervous about getting up and speaking — as I am sure most people there did — but I got up and expressed my love for her anyway. I was able to overcome my nervousness because I knew I didn't need to get it "right." All I had to do was express my heart's truth — and that's what counted. And that's what I did.

I shared with her how much I loved her, and how I appreciated how she had stuck by me and believed in me during the hard times I went through when I was younger. And then we hugged. Nothing complicated; but how great did it feel for me to have said it! And, I'm sure, equally great for my aunt to hear me stand before people and express my love and gratitude.

That's what I learned through Speak Truthfully: to be able to speak my heart's truth and express my love for others — rather than living with the regret of not saying what's in my heart to say.

Commentary

"I will not die an unlived life, I will not live in fear ..."
Dawna Markova

I must confess that when I first received John's essay, I was dismayed at its brevity. It's 368 words. Then, I read it.

I read it again. Then I sat in my chair, gazing out the window. I fell into a slow-motion life review of just such moments as John describes: opportunities to speak from my heart, to share my deep feelings of love and respect and gratitude for another person. In this regard, I have more missed opportunities than I am proud to admit.

The only time I ever saw my elder brother cry was shortly after our father died. He had died suddenly and unexpectedly. He was only 53. Family and friends had gathered at our house to comfort one another. I noticed my brother wander out to the back yard and then slip through the gate into the neighboring park. I went out and joined him. He was sitting cross-legged on the dirty grass, head down, sobbing. I don't remember specifically what we said, but it had something to do with the deep feelings for those we love which show up after a great loss. We said something about taking time to appreciate the people we love, about being present with them instead of speeding along on the freeways of our day-to-day mindless busyness. I'm sure we spoke of what people everywhere speak of when a father, mother, wife, husband, or child dies suddenly, unexpectedly — and we realize too late that there was something we wanted to say, but didn't; something we wanted to do, but didn't; some way we wanted to be, but weren't.

We realize too late ... we miss the opportunities ... for any number of reasons. At gatherings like John describes, maybe we'll hold back because of nervousness, or embarrassment, or discomfort with deep feeling and emotion. Maybe we're just not paying attention. Maybe we're drunk. Maybe we think, *I'll tell her tomorrow.*

I've come right to the edge of death a number of times, and each time the regrets that flash before me are missed opportunities to share my sweetness, to express my love, to speak from my heart to another's heart.

I'll stop right here, at exactly 368 words.

Do Your Lovin' Thing

Amy Tait

So there I was, standing in front of 60 people, knowing that I had something important to say and that I couldn't rely on anyone else to say it, when I was overcome with something … fear? Terror? It wasn't as obvious as that, but whatever it was almost paralyzed me. I became rooted to the spot and acutely aware of my vulnerability in front of all these people. Who the hell did I think I was? I couldn't do this! This was a room full of experts. I was new to the job. I was a young, blonde female and it was going to be transparent to everyone that I didn't know what I was talking about. So far in my career I had gotten away with what I thought of as my "big bluff" — managing to convince people I was capable, competent, and confident — but I was about to give myself away in one swift, mortifying public speaking moment. I felt the blood rush to my face, making my cheeks burn; then my voice cracked and wobbled and I cursed my body for betraying me in this brutal way. I knew the only way out was to finish, so I raced through my brief message and managed to get back to my seat, shaking, sweating and bitterly aware that I had just become a member of the group that I had long been determined not to join: the group of people who have a fear of public speaking.

I left that day with a steely determination that I was *not* going to surrender easily. Fear of public speaking was too much of a cliché — I couldn't stand it. I knew that if I wanted to go anywhere with my career I had to be a capable public speaker. If I wanted to inspire people, effect change and try to do some good in this world then I needed to be able to communicate without crumbling.

But what to do? I had done various training courses on presentation skills and public speaking and I knew all about voice projection, taking a walk before speaking, breathing techniques, slowing down … . Intellectually I knew all the tricks, so I wanted something else, something that ran deeper than physical strategies to overcome nerves and lack of confidence.

And that's when someone sent me a link to Robert Rabbin's website. I looked it up and almost cried with relief to discover that Robert's Speak Truthfully course offered something beyond "slow down, speak up, and you'll be right."

Three weeks later I was at the Speak Truthfully course. And I walked away from this course with more than some handy presentation tips. I walked away with a new confidence in my speaking ability, and a new perspective on myself and my life and the way I wanted to be. I felt invigorated. And I felt BIG.

I experienced four main breakthroughs over the weekend.

Firstly, early on in the course, Robert defined public speaking as "speaking to anyone other than yourself, regardless of circumstances or venue or purpose." I had never thought about it like that. I had always had two fairly distinct categories: speaking socially, and speaking professionally.

Speaking socially has always been something I'm comfortable with. I enjoy meeting people, getting to know them and gently drawing out their stories. Other people have always been of interest to me, and conversation usually comes easily — largely because I'm unafraid to show myself, and tell people about me, my life, my dreams, my fears, my embarrassing stories. Oh yes, socially, everything was hunky dory.

Speaking professionally, however, now *there* was my problem. This was where I always had to impress, felt under pressure to perform, and had to excel in order to overcome the fact that my audience would inevitably be thinking "she's so young and incapable" before I even opened my mouth.

But Robert had a different idea. He explained that speaking was just speaking; we need not divide it up like I had done. He said it is critical to connect authentically with the message and the audience regardless of the situation in which you're doing it — social or professional, what's the difference? After all, we are who we are, and if we can speak confidently in one area of life, then why not *all* areas? I saw how much I had been shying away from this in my professional life. I was so caught up in acting the part and proving myself that it was no wonder I couldn't convey a clear message. Socially I always ensured that *I* was part of the message, I always tried to connect with people authentically, but professionally I tried everything I could to make sure I *wasn't* part of the message. I wanted to be invisible, to hide my youth, so that my employers would think I was able.

Was it that simple? Yes. It really was. I realized that I knew how to speak — clearly, coherently, and persuasively. I just did it in a social context better than I did it in a professional one. Robert filmed us speaking and I watched the film dumbfounded, as I saw myself being entertaining and articulate, and genuinely engaging. I remember being struck by the fact that I wasn't as bad as I thought. I was actually quite good! I was sad that I had spent so much time being so mean to myself! So I just needed to take that to work with me, I just needed to turn my social speaking skills into professional speaking skills. I knew that if I started to connect authentically at work, the rest would follow.

I was zapped with my second breakthrough when Robert

demonstrated to all of us how words just "arrive." I had let my professional speaking nervousness fool me into thinking that I didn't know what to say, or that I'd get lost and forget what I had rehearsed. If you give yourself the space and time, whatever you need to say will bubble up to the surface, ready to be said. Again, I saw how I trusted this in social settings: I don't arrive at dinner parties with a notebook of pre-planned conversation starters or a list titled "handy things to say in the event of an awkward moment." In social situations, conversation ebbs and flows and I am comfortable to just let that happen. At work, and particularly in meetings, it was a whole other story. In meetings I would turn words over and over in my mind before I plucked up the courage to say them (often, in fact, taking too long and missing the opportunity to speak!). I would try and plan my comments to sound as erudite as possible, so as not to humiliate myself or anyone with me by being inarticulate. I greatly feared that I would inspire the embarrassed silence that comes after someone has said something shockingly obvious/stupid/off-the-point.

Robert pointed out how differently I was approaching this aspect of my life and I was shocked that I had never noticed it myself. I realized that meetings, basically, were just like dinner parties! If I have something to say, I can trust that if I open my mouth and connect authentically, it will be said, and it will be said however it needs to be said.

Again, this sounds pretty simple but for me it was revolutionary.

Breakthrough number three was a biggie. Once the realization had dawned on me that I had not been present in my speaking at work, I saw how I had, for all intents and purposes, been pretending I was someone else. In my professional world of senior, white, learned, (mostly) males, professionally I was doing everything I could to *not* be who I am; I was trying hard to *not* be young, to *not* be female and to *not* be blonde. I even wore my glasses when I didn't need to so I'd look smarter! I saw how futile this was, how completely daft. I *am* young, I *am* female, and I *am* blonde. Trying to be otherwise is a heck of a wasted effort and I'm unlikely to fool anyone. However, I am also smart and fun and engaging. So *all* of that needs to be a part of my message.

Robert showed me how people will always judge me and that I can't do anything about that, but that it's actually kind of cool for people to be thinking "wow, she's young," while I speak to them through my heart.

Which brings me to breakthrough number four. At the end of the course, we had to give a speech about what matters to us most. I spoke about love. Because it really does matter to me most. Over the past three years I have had an amazing journey with my heart, and with learning the joyful art of loving. I told the group openly and shamelessly about my experiences, and the fun I had had splashing my love around to friends, family and pretty much anyone who got in its way.

As I spoke, I noticed that I hadn't talked about this for a while. It felt like I was dusting off a favorite toy that I had forgotten was on the shelf. I hadn't hung out with my heart very much, it had sort of faded into the background, which surprised me because there was a time when it was a real focus for me. It was so exciting to connect with it again, even just for that two minute speech. Breakthrough number four showed me how to get my heart back into my voice.

On Monday, back in the office, I had to go into a meeting with 15 senior people to present on aspects of a national project. For the first time in my life, I couldn't wait to get in there. I left my glasses off (I didn't need them!) and just sat in the meeting talking with people as Amy, and all the things that she means: vulnerable, capable, young, silly, interested, interesting, not-particularly-fashionable, tertiary educated, brave, insecure, short, witty, confused, responsible and questioning, with blue eyes, blonde hair, and big cheeks.

I was just me, and it was fine. I was fine! In fact it was very amusing to me that nobody else was noticing the quiet revolution that was taking place at the top end of the boardroom. It is so wonderful to have me back.

Commentary

"Hey, love and mercy — that's what you need tonight.
So, love and mercy to you and your friends tonight."
Brian Wilson

We can only speak from our heart if we know our heart, if we are unafraid to do our lovin' thing! This deep connection to our feelings, especially to love, is what elevates and beautifies our speaking beyond any technique or skill.

In the workshops, I assign all kinds of talk topics. Somewhere around the halfway mark, I almost always say, "Give a three-minute talk beginning with *What I love most in the world is …* . If people start too fast, or if I think they're too in their head, I stop them. "Saturate each word with the feeling of love. Don't describe, demonstrate. Feel it. Show it. If tears come, let them come. If your feeling overwhelms you, if you can't speak because of the emotion, then stand there without speaking, and just show us the emotion." I'll tell a story or two of how I've sat on a stage in front of hundreds of people, and cried. I'm not telling them to do this, or that they should. I'm asking them to consider that showing our true emotions can be a part of our speaking. We do not have to bury these feelings, or be afraid of them, or manage them. We do not have to fear them. We can let them be a part of our speaking.

It never fails. These talks are dramatically different than their earlier talks. Something happens to them through this connection to their love for someone, or something. Their face is brighter, their rate of speech slows down, the quality of their connection is vastly stronger. They stop hiding. They become, in a word, real. They become present. They become beautiful and inspiring speakers.

I emphasize the importance of speaking from the heart. I want people to see for themselves that when they settle into themselves and talk about things that matter to them, when they open their heart to the audience, when they are unafraid of deeply feeling and showing the emotion of "what I love," I want them to see how transformative this. I want them to see what happens when they speak from their heart.

There is an intoxicating freedom and power in this realization that we do not have to fear our heart. We do not have to fear our capacity to feel our speaking, to put our feelings into our speaking. Yes, even in business! Even in government policy-making agencies!

I never tell people how they should speak, or what they should say. That is up to them. I do, however, say that unless we are free to choose, unless we are able to say what we want, we are not free. It is our fear that chooses. I am not afraid to sit on a stage and sob. I am not saying you should. I am not even saying it is correct, or right, or appropriate. I am saying that is what I am willing to do. I am saying it is my choice to do that. I can only choose to not do that, if I am free to do it. I just want people to be able to freely choose how to speak, what to say, and how to say it.

OK, fine, I admit it. I do have a preference for people, like Amy, who are willing to speak their lovin' thing! It makes my heart pound and my head spin.

At the end of most workshops, I stage a very modest "ritual." I ask each person, one at a time, to come to the front and sit in front of the others. I invite people to consider their experience of the person sitting before them, and to acknowledge them for something they admired, enjoyed, or appreciated about that person's participation. Then, I give each person a certificate of completion. I might say a word or two if I'm so moved.

I remember looking at Amy, sitting at the front of the room, receiving the appreciative comments of the other participants. Then, it was my turn. I stood. I was filled with the feeling of Amy's talks and of how she put her heart right out there for all of us to see. I said, "Amy, don't be afraid of your heart, and of how much love you have inside you to give to the world." Then I hugged her and gave her the certificate.

Thank you, Amy, for doing your lovin' thing.

Sing Your Own Song

Sky Shayne Innes

"The greatest gift you can give another is the purity of your attention."
Richard Moss

"If I turn now I will be *dead*, and then I won't have to perform tomorrow!"

Fear disguised as desperation wanted to, but some life-preserving instinct made me push down on the accelerator hard and savagely, and I shot across, escaping a full head-on by a whisker. Like a tsunami, adrenalin drowned my body and I pulled over in the wooded gloom of a country road until the shaking stilled. I listened to that poor truck driver in the dark with all his hundreds of nightlights, still blasting his horn as he headed down the Pacific Highway. Little would he have been expecting that brief death dance with a mad woman. Shame and exhilaration vied with each other.

"How could I do that to him? How could I do that to my self? I'm still *alive!*"

Yes, exhilaration to be alive but my heart sinking because, as I am alive, I have a presentation to do tomorrow.

This event happened ten years ago and represents the abyss of my fear of presentation and public speaking. Needless to say, my performance the next day was, if not a total failure, pretty poor. After that experience I became even more terrified of public speaking and found every trick in the book to avoid it at all costs.

There is a hilarious quote from the comedian Jerry Seinfeld in Robert's workbook, which captures not only my fear, but many people's fear of public speaking. He says, "According to most studies, people's number one fear is public speaking. Number two is death. Death is number two. Does that sound right? This means that when an average person goes to a funeral, they'd rather be in the casket than delivering the eulogy!"

Why do so many of us have such fear? Regardless of the many different permutations, the fear is always about *being*: being seen, being heard — and somehow failing in this way of being. And yet, every day of our lives we are being seen and heard. As Robert points out, regardless of whether we give lectures and presentations, we are all public speakers. Every day we are "presenting" ourselves in one way or another, be it expressing our point of view at the dinner table or at a job interview. Sadly, for some of us the fear of public speaking can be so great it affects our career choice, determines the opportunities we accept or decline, and limits our achievements, because we are afraid of some form of public speaking. How sad that very special occasions of happiness and celebration, like birthdays and weddings, become occasions of great distress if we are required to give a speech.

Many of us would like to avoid this problem entirely, but the truth is we can't. As Robert says, "There is no such thing as a private speaker. Public speaking occurs whenever you speak to anyone other than yourself—whether it be to one or one thousand. And every public speaking encounter is an opportunity for us to show who we are." If we do avoid this form of expression, we can be sure that in some way we are limiting ourselves and our ability to have full and meaningful lives. For, the gift we have for each other is the unique and idiosyncratically individual expression that each one of us is. I am passionate about my work. Years ago, a client of mine, a journalist, asked me what it is that I love so much about my work. Something in the authenticity of her question caused me to consider deeply this question that was to become so significant.

Let me explain. When I was much, much younger, I had an abiding question: "Why am I the way I am?" This question plagued me so much that after leaving school I went to university and studied psychology to find out. Needless to say I didn't find any real answers, but in asking the question I came to discover the extraordinary mystery of who I am and who you are. This mystery includes fourteen billion years of creation and evolution. What an extraordinary work of consciousness you are, we are, it all is! And, most excitingly, it is a work in progress. Now I no longer look for an answer but relish the exploration of the mystery. "Why" became "how" and the how was all about change and evolving and becoming all that we may be. As I say in my book, *Love's Alchemy*, "The divine purpose of existence is to unfold in the expression that I am."

This is the work I do, for myself and with other people. I work with people who are deeply interested in growth and in excellence. At this point you may well say, "It is obvious why you love your work." Nonetheless, this timely question gave me cause to consider beyond the obvious and go deeper.

I love the work I do because it gives me the opportunity to *connect*. This not very startling word has, at its heart, a vitally important component of our being. Most of the ills of our world are from a lack of real connection. We feel separate and quite often alone. We meet each other, yes, but we meet behind layers of protection and a myriad of "happy face" masks. Our communication keeps us safe and as invulnerable as we can make ourselves.

In other words, we hide. Not only do we hide from each other but also we hide from ourselves. Our communication, our public speaking, is a lie. It presents who we think we should be rather than who we really are.

Connection, on the other hand, is heart to heart communication. It is recognizing ourselves in each other and reaching out to that. It may be anything from our wisdom to our hurt but it is always a recognition of the human condition, which we all share. In my work I am able to connect with people in very real ways that are often considered too meaningful or personal for ordinary discourse. The importance of such a dialogue is to share so that something that is not yet present is evoked. This is the significance of the coaching or therapeutic conversation. And speaking from the heart is how real connection happens.

Given my passion for real connection and communication, why would I be so frightened of public speaking? Through Robert's seminar I came to understand precisely why. Even though a significant awareness of my spiritual and philosophical inquiry is informed by our intrinsic connectedness, I stopped feeling connected when I was expected to deliver the message. Instead, I felt deeply disconnected and very separate. I felt I had to be brilliant, perfect, and all knowing. If I weren't I would be failing my audience and they would be bored and disappointed. They wouldn't get the message they had come for. I would have failed miserably, feeling embarrassed and utterly humiliated. Little wonder my knees would shake uncontrollably. Oh, and how further mortifying!

What I was overlooking is that *I am the message* and it is none of my business how they receive the message. That's their business. My business is to be the message as authentically and truly as I can. This means to communicate from my heart, from my very essence. In my work I know this so well, but the moment I label the message as public speaking, I trap myself in the delusion of who I think I should be rather than being who I truly am. I become someone other than me; I try to be this so-called public speaker rather than me.

No matter how erudite or articulate your presentation may be, if it is communicated without you, it will probably be boring and have little value. Years ago I remember hearing a lecture on the Mandelbrot equation and fractals. I hardly understood a scientific word that was spoken, but I walked away thrilled and elated. His passion had given me a sense of the nature of reality and an experience of what infinity really means. This was his unique gift of expression experienced just as uniquely by me. This is connection. This is communication. I learned that this is what public speaking is all about.

That question all those years ago from my journalist client clarified one of the most important aspects of my work. More than anything I can say or do, the connection between my client and me is what weaves the magic carpet carrying us forward to transformed landscapes. Developing a rich and powerful connection allows real growth and creativity. It is love in action. It honors and values us exactly as we are and out of that we access our wisdom. We develop congruence between our unique expression and its delivery.

Robert's course clarified another aspect. It was the words "YOU are the message" on his brochure which overrode my fear and got me there. A radical sage he must be to know such a thing! With these words my heart leapt in recognition of the truth. The gift I received from his teaching is to do away with the unhelpful distinction of public speaking being something that happens with an "audience." What is an audience? It is just people, and unless there is connection there is no authentic communication.

There is a wonderful story that comes out of Africa. In this particular tribe, a pregnant woman goes into the wilderness with her friends until they have the song of the child. When the child is born, the community sings this very special song to the child. Thereafter the song is sung only for initiation into adulthood, marriage, and finally at the person's deathbed.

There is one other occasion when the villagers sing this song. If at any time the person commits a crime, the villagers gather and sing his song to remind him of who he is.

Thank you, Robert, for singing my song and reminding me of who I am in those "public speaking" moments when I had forgotten. Now I am happily, outrageously, and exuberantly singing my own song.

My song, my vision, is for the concept of love's alchemy to be as commonly understood as mother's love. As Mother Teresa said, the biggest disease today is the lack of love. Until we know the power of love, we are doomed to leave a legacy of self-seeking destruction.

My inspiration is our call as humanity to awaken to the true purpose we are here to fulfill. This is not a noble endeavor but a practical and realistic way of living our lives fully and bountifully in whatever way that means to us. For in our fulfillment is our purpose and our evolution. This is the way of love's alchemy and you are the alchemist.

Commentary

"The most essential thing in life is to establish an unafraid, heartfelt communication with others."
Sogyal Rinpoche

I love Sky's African story! "… the villagers gather and sing his song to remind him of who he is."

I've talked a lot about authenticity and transparency and vulnerability and connection in this book, lots of words about what may still seem like high-minded or remote, maybe even unreachable, ideas. We've seen in Carla's essay that even after years in a convent and a lifetime of self-exploration, we can still come to a flimsy floor, a new wound, another falsehood. Is real authenticity even possible? Can we speak our truth if we don't know it or if we've forgotten it? Can we be authentic if we don't know who we are?

"Who am I?" is a seminal life question, isn't it? It is both mystical and practical, otherworldly and this-worldly, philosophical and pragmatic. It's everything. After all, if YOU are the message, than who, or what, are YOU?

Sky's story reminds me of one of my favorite poems, by the Indian poet Kabir, especially this muscular and modern translation by Robert Bly, "We sense that there is some sort of spirit that loves birds and animals and the ants — perhaps the same one who gave a radiance to you in your mother's womb. Is it logical you would be walking around entirely orphaned now? The truth is you turned away yourself and decided to go into the dark alone. Now you are tangled up in others and have forgotten what you once knew, and that's why everything you do has some weird failure in it."

It may be too big a statement to say that this forgetting "what we once knew" is the mischief that makes us think we can't speak our truth credibly, confidently, courageously. But it may not be.

After inspecting all the clues and available evidence, I think it is not too big a statement; it is just right. If we could all remember what we once knew, what we do know way down deep, beneath the busy mind and flimsy floors of shame, behind the masks and roles and distortions and defenses — way down, right down to the core of our innocence and clarity — we'd not need the singing to remind us. We'd be the song.

When I was eleven years old, I lived with my family in Torino, Italy. I had broken my leg in a skiing accident in Cervino, the Italian side of the Matterhorn. In bed for a month, I read the encyclopedia. I was particularly taken with the entries dealing with the origins and dimensions and mysteries of the cosmos. One day, my head all turned around and inside out from incessant reading and dreaming, a spirit filled the room. When it left, I reverberated with the question, Who am I?

For years, I followed that question around the world, exploring outside and inside, looking for the answer. Finally, I found it. Problem is, I can't really say what I found, because the answer came in the huge high mountains of pure silence. Every time I try to say what I found, I fail before a sound comes out. But I did find out. I remembered what I once knew. I heard the song. I knew, and know, who I am.

That's why I love silence. Not the silence of no noise or sound, but the silence of the beginning of time, before anything existed, before anything was born. Kabir wrote about this silence. He said, "I reached the place inside me where the world is breathing." That kind of silence.

Silence is where we find ourselves and where we find each other. In this silence, we remember what we once knew, and we hear the song of who we are. That's all we need. The rest pretty much takes care of itself. We do have to show up and play the game, but when we find out who we are in silence, we aren't confused or lost or afraid anymore. That makes all the difference in the world, doesn't it?

Only this morning, I was with a client who came to me because he wants to speak more slowly, so he said. He is tops in his field, technically, but he speaks too fast to be effective. He doesn't listen that well. He doesn't create connection, without which there is no trust. He is a leader, and he knows that if people don't trust him, his leadership integrity will be compromised. He knows that he barks, rather than speaks. People are tentative around him. They approach warily. After a few minutes of this morning's session, our first, he confessed, "It's really hard to listen to you. You speak so slowly! It's really frustrating." You've got to love that! I told him that the entire issue was not slow or fast, but presence and awareness.

I do have a distinctive style of speaking. I don't think of it in terms of slow or fast. I think of it in terms of being aware of what I'm saying while I'm saying it. I speak slow and fast, but never too slow or too fast to obscure silence, to dim or darken real-time awareness. I learned to speak the way I do in silence. In my workshops, I don't talk about the "pause" that conventional public speaking courses talk about. I talk about silence. Pause is a technique. Silence is a state of being. In the ashram where I lived for ten years, silence was OK. It was a good thing to be quiet and still, but then again we didn't have much else to do. When I left the ashram and entered corporate America as a consultant, I noticed that people had so much to do they were *never* quiet or still. I wondered if anyone knew about silence, about what we once knew, about the song of who we are.

After I published my first book, my publicist secured my very first radio interview. I've done many since then, but that one was precious because I lost my on-air virginity. I didn't know about the dreaded "dead air." It's radio, honey, and people want to listen to *something*! Who knew? My publicist came up to me after and very softly, afraid of offending me, tried to clue me in to this fact. He said, "Robert, you've got to get over this silence thing. People want to hear you. You've got to speak faster. The silence thing doesn't work on radio." I get that a lot. Except it does work, on radio and everywhere else.

I once waited so long to answer a question from an audience member during a public lecture that people became concerned. From about the third or fourth row, I heard a voice say, "Um, Robert, if it's OK, I think I know the answer." I said I was just having an extended senior moment, which may have been the case. When I finally did answer the question, I was of course brilliant as always.

I never lose touch with silence. I need silence to breathe, to live, to function. Silence is a meditative state of real-time awareness. It's outside, but includes, our thought-stream. Silence, however, does not make us passive and indrawn; it frees us from doubt and distractions so we can be focused, active, and dynamic. I am neither slow moving nor slow thinking. I'm hugely capable, effective, and efficient. I was once given a blank check by a corporate client to produce a three-day company-wide retreat. He didn't want to know anything about it. He just said, "I know you'll do the right thing. I trust you." The retreat ended up costing over a million dollars. On top of my fees, he gave me a very expensive watch as a further "thank you" because he was so happy with the event. My capability, my imagination, my everything came, and comes, from silence.

Silence is not just the spiritual place where we remember what we once knew about ourselves, it is not just the place where we hear the song of ourselves — it is the place of practicality and pragmatism, mixed with just the right amount of magic! I could tell you many stories about the efficacy of silence, but that's another book.

For now, I want to say that silence is all-important in our speaking. Silence is a wish-fulfilling tree, a gift-giving giant. Our friendship with silence bestows many benefits. Silence connects us to ourselves and to others, heart to heart. Silence liberates our authentic feelings and passions so they can enrich our words. Silence keeps our eyes clean and clear so that when people look into these windows, they truly see our soul. Silence is our real-time speaking navigator, telling us exactly where we are and plotting an unerring course to where we want to go. Silence is the awareness of what we are saying and how we are saying it, *while* we are saying it. Silence is self-awareness, it is intuition, it is spontaneity. Silence is listening, and we must listen as we speak. Without listening there is no speaking, there is only broadcasting. Silence is complete comfort in front of the room, and when we are comfortable we can more easily choose confidence. Silence creates comfort and confidence, which will defeat anxiety and doubt at every turn.

Many people tell me about their fears of being asked a question they can't answer, or of losing their train of thought, or of forgetting something they want to say, of blacking out on their feet. Many people talk "too fast" because they are afraid of simply standing in front of people, afraid of seeing and being seen. They speak fast and nonstop to hide, to distract, to defend.

The antidote to all this distress is silence. I ask people to let stillness come into them. I ask people to be aware of their breathing, even as they speak. A woman in a recent workshop said, after one of her talks, "I forgot to breathe." It was a five-minute talk, so you do the math. She didn't forget to breathe, she forgot to notice that she was breathing! Silence is there in our breath. Silence is there in the spaces between the words. I ask people to speak being mindful of the spaces between words on a page. Ifldon'thitthespaceb arafterevery word, you wouldn't be able to read one page! If we don't put a space between our spoken words, and between sentences, it is the same kind of gibberish. From those mindful spaces, silence comes into us of its own. When silence comes into our speaking, we are always comfortable, relaxed, unafraid, unhurried and aware of what we are saying while we are saying it. We speak consciously, creatively, clearly.

Speak Truthfully is a gift to me from silence, and I offer it to you.

Contributor Biographies

Özlem Beldan
www.ozlembeldan.com
Following a 15-year career in international corporate financial management, Özlem launched her own business, coaching and mentoring women to bring meaning and motivation to their money management. She has poured her experience, knowledge, and skills into her Conscious Money program, designed specifically to support women in improving their financial literacy and to assist them in achieving their personal and business goals and dreams. Özlem is a licensed RealTime Speaking and Meaning and Motivation facilitator.

Shakaya Leone
www.earthempress.com
Shakaya Leone is a blissful wife and mother and an inspired voice in the natural health and raw food community. Shakaya says, “You are beautiful and brilliant. You walk a path no one else could walk.” Shakaya can be found barefoot in the forest or swimming in the ocean or conjuring a new elixir of love and health in her kitchen.

Carla van Raay
www.carlavanraay.com
Carla is the author of God’s Callgirl, her memoir of how she became free from her past, and Desire: Awakening God’s Woman. She is a Theta Healer and Light-Energy worker, and is passionate about bringing abundant life to those people over 40, which she does through seminars and personal programs designed to heal sabotaging patterns.

Laurent S. Labourmène
www.labourmene.com
Laurent is a leadership advisor and mentor, an award winning social entrepreneur and a ‘maven’ and ‘connector’ for world-changing people and world-changing ideas.

Sherrie Hatfield
www.sherriehatfield.com
Sherrie is a certified advanced practitioner and senior trainer in the Mace Energy Method and the first licensee of Speak Truthfully. She is guided by the core principles of integrity, truthfulness, simplicity, practicality, and playfulness. Sherrie is married, has three grown children, three grandchildren, and lives in Australia in the Gold Coast Hinterland.

Caroline Power
Caroline is a recent transplant to New York City, and is focusing on bringing her spirit to life and having fun in the world!

Hermine Zielinski
Hermine recently left her job as an IT helpdesk manager at a global organization so she could gallop with horses and fly with eagles — literally! Hermine's favorite pastimes include horse riding and hang-gliding.

Lou Bacher
www.adaptivethinking.com.au
Lou has spent more than 30 years as a GM, MD, and CEO in a variety of industries. He is currently founder and principal consultant of Adaptive Thinking, a training and consulting company offering guidance and support for managers and executives in leadership, management, communication, and public speaking.

Dana Carr
Dana keeps busy with bookwork for her family's carpet company as well as doing fund-raising for her children's school. She and her husband are parents of three beautiful children, three cats, two dogs, four goldfish, and one little bird.

Linley Anderson
Linley is a teacher in a primary school, helping children to see their own inner beauty. She is practices Huna Massage, Reiki, Transcendental Meditation, and Reconnective Healing. Her journey led her to her partner Chris and together they continue their travels outward and inward.

Kate Bezar
www.dumbofeather.com
Kate is the creator of a mook (magazine-book hybrid) called Dumbo feather, a quarterly publication filled with tales of passionate people making positive contributions to society. These stories have helped Kate on her quest to find what she is passionate about, which for now is keeping Dumbo feather going.

Michael Jensen
www.c4mconsultants.com.au
Starting out as a corporate banking lawyer, Michael decided at age 30 that he was better suited as a mediator of conflicts and disputes, mainly in the workplace. When not mediating disputes, he and his wife assist a charitable foundation called RunForYourLife, offering practical support to people living with cancer and their caregivers.

Suzanne Saad
www.breathehr.com.au
Suzanne is a registered practitioner and introductory teacher of the Aura-Soma color system. She runs her own business called breathe:HR, offering motivation and well-being workshops and consultations to help people find their own personal source of meaning in their lives and work.

Lynn Berry
The common thread running through the many careers Lynn has had is teaching, whether it be swimming, academic writing, or organizational communication. She also enjoys Reiki, iridology, shamanic drumming, and Ayurvedic cooking, as well as gardening, walking, going for long drives, and swimming like a dolphin.

Nicole Lloyd
www.soundbirth.com.au
Nicole is a licensed Simply Music teacher, working from her home in the Perth hills while also attending university to complete a Dip-Ed in Early Childhood Studies. She is also the founder of SoundBirth, supporting women to have empowering, natural birth experiences

Margaret Gill
www.margaretgill.com
After years of personal and spiritual development, challenges, and learning, Margaret realized her dream and founded her own company called Abundant Private Practices dedicated to positively helping others. Her passion is helping natural therapists build their clientele and achieve remarkable business results.

Michelle Wilson
www.relinque.com.au
Michelle has been an osteopath for more than 10 years, a profession she finds both challenging and rewarding. She and her husband opened Relinque Health Center, an osteopathic clinic, where they assist people to enjoy life without pain. Michelle and Adam recently became first-time parents.

Adam Wilson
www.relinque.com.au
Adam is an osteopath in Melbourne. Along with his wife Michelle, Adam opened Relinque Health Center, an osteopathic clinic. He loves skiing, and has even traveled to Japan in search of great slopes. He and Michelle recently became first-time parents.

Ida Lyall
www.idalyall.com
Ida is a holistic healer, holding certificates in kinesiology, Avatar system, Mastery in Theta, Transforming Memories in Theta and Delta, Sekhem Healing, and hypnotherapy. Her core philosophy is that the true healing of illness, disease, and imbalance in life requires a holistic approach, and as such she integrates a variety of modalities to work with the body, mind, emotions, and spirit in order to change a client's total state of being.

Bianca Pickett
www.employeeecosystem.com.au
Bianca helped grow one of Australia's premier IT companies, in the role of IT HR manager. She has recently founded her own consulting and training company to help her clients create and maintain high level of employee engagement. She also paints, sings, reads; is a triathlete, a healer, a writer; and a lover of all things quirky.

John Anderson
www.conversionmasters.com.au
John is a product launch expert. He works closely with business owners in the areas of health and wellness, business development, and property and investment services.

Amy Tait
Amy currently works for the Department of the Attorney General, helping to develop policy in the area of social justice. She loves the beach, the bush, the stars, and her family, and looks forward to discovering what the universe has in store for her next.

Sky Shayne Innes
www.lovesalchemy.com
The author of Love's Alchemy, Sky likes to describe herself as an alchemist, one who speaks about the transformative power of love. When not at home with her partner John, she travels about, experiencing life's diverse and delicious fare and giving talks on love's powerful alchemy.

Robert Rabbin

After more than 15 years of intensive meditation and self-inquiry, Robert began his distinctive professional journey in 1985. Since then, he has developed an international reputation as a groundbreaking speaker, self-awareness teacher, and leadership adviser. He is the creator of RealTime Speaking and Authenticity Accelerator.

Robert has published eight books and more than 200 articles on the themes of meditation, self-inquiry, leadership, public speaking, authentic self-expression, and spiritual activism. He was commissioned to write original essays for three leading-edge anthologies and was interviewed for *The Awakening West,* a collection of conversations with contemporary Western wisdom teachers.

Robert now travels the world offering Authenticity Accelerator programs, in which he teaches people how to understand, use, and apply The 5 Principles of Authentic Living:

Be Present
Pay Attention
Listen Deeply
Speak Truthfully
Act Creatively

To contact Robert, and for detailed information about his work, please visit his websites:

www.AuthenticityAccelerator.com

Authenticity Accelerator Programs

The **Authenticity Accelerator** is Robert's flagship program, a launch pad to an authentic life, an adventure into the heart of authentic living and speaking. The **Authenticity Accelerator** is an exploration of living with courage and confidence, intimacy and vulnerability, honesty and transparency — and a discovery of each person's capacity to create a truly authentic life.

The **Authenticity Accelerator** is available to individuals, groups, communities, teams, and organizations in a variety of formats, including:

- half-day seminars
- one-day workshops
- multi-day retreats
- individual coaching
- 90-minute presentations.

Speak Truthfully Programs

Robert offers five programs for people who truly want to develop and refine their ability to speak truthfully — with confidence, credibility, and authentic connection. Speaking Truthfully is the first bridge we cross as we bring forth our deep truth and heart from the inner to the outer world. It is how we begin to make our authentic impulses real in our lives, how we begin to see an accurate and liberating reflection of these impulses in our choices, actions, relationships, and work.

Speak Truthfully
Speaking with Your Authentic Voice

Confidence is a Choice
Reclaiming Your Power to Speak and Be Heard

YOU Are the Message
Speaking with Credibility, Confidence, and Connection

Speak for Effect
Creating Clear, Concise, and Compelling Content

Conscious Communication in the Workplace
Creating a Culture of Truthful Speaking

If you would like to sponsor a public program or bring Authenticity Accelerator or Speak Truthfully to your organization, please contact Robert.

Additional Products

The following products by Robert Rabbin are available through the Store on the Authenticity Accelerator website, as well as through many online resellers.

Paperback

- *The 5 Principles of Authentic Living: How to Live an Authentic Life in 10 Words*
- *Speak Truthfully: Speak Your Way to an Authentic Life with Awareness, Courage, and Confidence*
- *Sound Bites from Silence: Scouting Reports from the Frontier of Consciousness*
- *The Explosive Silence of Meditation: 48 Sutras for Modern Mystics*
- *The Guillotine of Silence: It's Never How You Think It Is*
- *Radical Wisdom: Living from Silence while Rocking the World*
- *A Mystic in Corporate America*

E-Books

- *The 5 Principles of Authentic Living: How to Live an Authentic Life in 10 Words*
- *Speak Truthfully: Speak Your Way to an Authentic Life with Awareness, Courage, and Confidence*
- *Sound Bites from Silence: Scouting Reports from the Frontier of Consciousness*
- *The Explosive Silence of Meditation: 48 Sutras for Modern Mystics*
- *The Guillotine of Silence: It's Never How You Think It Is*
- *A Mystic in Corporate America*
- *Radical Sages: An Evolution of Spiritual Activism*
- *The Meaning and Motivation Workbook*

Audiobooks

- *The 5 Principles of Authentic Living: How to Live an Authentic Life in 10 Words*
- *Igniting Your Soul at Work: Unleashing Authentic Insight and Action*
- *Sound Bites from Silence: Scouting Reports from the Frontier of Consciousness*
- *Radical Wisdom: Living from Silence while Rocking the World*

CPSIA information can be obtained at www.ICGtesting.com
Printed in the USA
LVOW081944210513

334869LV00002B/556/P